CHAOS *to* CONNECTION™

9 Heart-Centered Essentials *for* Parenting Your Teen

CHAOS TO CONNECTION ™

9 Heart-Centered Essentials for Parenting Your Teen

Published by Vive, Inc.

207 Canyon Blvd, Suite 202, Boulder, CO 80302

www.ViveNow.com

First Edition

ISBN: 978-0-9825121-5-9

Printed in the United States of America

Designed by The Tenfold Collective

www.TenfoldCollective.com

TABLE OF CONTENTS

WELCOME

Welcome to *Chaos to Connection: 9 Heart-Centered Essentials for Parenting Your Teen.*

Welcome to the beginning of an entirely new way of relating to yourself and those you love to bring peace and calm to your home.

We congratulate you for using *Chaos to Connection* and for your willingness to seek support. We at Vive are excited about the opportunity to join you and your family on this journey of growth. Vive has worked with thousands of families, and many resemble yours. Originally a small company that started over ten years ago, Vive now has many passionate and experienced practitioners connecting with families in communities across the country. The nine heart-centered essentials were developed through these practitioners' extensive experience in healing and strengthening families. We are excited to be able to share these parenting essentials with many more families like yours.

Chaos to Connection will help you learn not so much how to avoid chaos but how to change from being paralyzed to connecting in the chaos. By "connecting," we mean really knowing or starting the journey of knowing another person. Connection is when the truest part of your heart meets the emptiest recesses in another and finds something there worth exploring. Connection like this leaves the initiator fuller than before, and the receiver feeling less terrified and, eventually, eager to experience an even deeper connection. Such a meeting of hearts is profound and natural, because we are wired to thrive in relationships. Our whole heart, body and mind crave connection.

You are capable of connecting to others, and connecting is of the utmost importance to you and those you love. It is only through authentic and honest connection that we can heal personally, help heal each other, and share that healing in our families.

The key component here is you. You in your entirety. You can start learning the fundamentals in *Chaos to Connection* by honestly getting to know all of you, looking at who you are, your life experience, what brings you happiness, what drives you crazy. By doing this, you will grow as a person and be able to get to know others better because you know yourself better. Remember this: the best way to help your child is to help yourself.

With this in mind, we include with *Chaos to Connection* a "Never Alone Guarantee." We at Vive promise to support you in this learning and growing process. Whenever you need it—in the heat of a chaotic moment, while driving your car, while lying in bed awake at night—support is always available to you by calling our support telephone number, 866-645-1781.

Our desire is that in the midst of chaos, you begin to feel relief and then excitement about what you will learn. These concepts *are* exciting, because they really work, in real life, with real families. And remember, you are never alone. We are here to help you every step of the way.

May you discover the joy of heart-centered parenting,

Vive, Inc.

START HERE

You are most likely experiencing a chaotic or turbulent time in your family. You may be trying to help a teen with any number of challenging behaviors. You are a loving, conscientious parent and want to know what you can do to help your child.

We want you to know that whatever you are going through—however dark and desperate this time in your family is—there is hope. Heart-centered parenting has the power to transform you, your family, and your relationships. You have taken an important step toward building a healthier family in choosing to read *Chaos to Connection: 9 Heart-Centered Essentials for Parenting Your Teen.*

We have healed and strengthened many families through direct services and the power of the nine heart-centered essentials. The concepts in *Chaos to Connection* are new and ground-breaking, but they are also proven and entirely attainable. We have every faith that you can use these new concepts to transform your life, connect with your child's heart, and be the parent you've always dreamed of. Now is the time for you to rediscover the joy of being a family.

Start Here will help you understand the foundations of *Chaos to Connection* and the nine essentials. We will introduce you to the concept of heart-centered parenting, possibly surprise you with the best way to help your child, give you a brief summary of the nine heart-centered essentials, and give you a little guidance on how to use this book.

You may be wondering what heart-centered parenting is. A common misconception of heart-centered parenting is that it involves giving in to a child's every whim. Heart-centered parenting is not about excusing or passively accepting a child's behavior. Heart-centered parenting is based on the beliefs that:

- An unconditionally loving connection and relationship with your child is more important and more healing than anything else, more important than how your teen behaves, what your teen does in the future, where your teen is living, or what your teen uses to be happy. Your relationship with your child is crucial.
- At our core, we are capable of and designed to thrive in loving relationships.
- All behaviors, no matter how dysfunctional, have an informative message behind them.
- Only through authentic and honest connection can we heal personally and heal each other.
- Parents must take responsibility for their feelings and needs in order to unconditionally love their child.
- Parenting and your relationship with your child is a process, one that embraces transitions and finds a way to connect despite the chaos of life.
- Parents are loving leaders in the lives of their teen.
- Everything you need in order to be a heart-centered parent, you already have.

Heart-centered parenting evolved from parents like you who looked to others for support in how to parent their children. Conventional parenting models concentrate on the child's behavior and changing that behavior through consequences. Heart-centered parenting understands that in the end, parents cannot control their child's behavior and views the child's behavior as exactly as it should be for the moment. Knowing that parents cannot control behavior, parents realize that their relationship with their child and the opportunity to be a loving presence is what truly matters.

What often occurs in conventional parenting is that the teen becomes the parent or even the "CEO" of feelings in the home. Parents who try to control their teen's behavior do so based on feelings of fear, shame, and judgment—fear for their child's safety or future, shame about their child's behavior, or judgment that their child is wrong. Controlling the teen then becomes about helping the parent to feel better, not about connecting and healing the relationship. When the control and power of the parent stops working, parents feel out of control and powerless, as if there's nothing they can do. For the teen, the relationship feels unsafe because she doesn't want to be responsible for her parents' feelings. Each one of us, though, is fully responsible for our own feelings and responsible for interacting with others from a place of connection rather than chaos. *Chaos to Connection* will help you to shift how you view your teen's behavior and your emotions to become empowered again.

Chaos to Connection does not provide a skill set of parenting techniques to show you how to change. It does provide the support you need to unconditionally love your child. Such a change in what you focus on may seem counter-intuitive, but it is, in fact, the connection with your child that makes the difference in your child's life. Shifting your focus is not a complex idea, but it does take time and practice.

Because the basis of heart-centered parenting is so different from conventional parenting, success in heart-centered parenting also looks different. You may be used to success looking like reaching a goal of "My child is obedient and does not do anything wrong." In heart-centered parenting, success is replaced by a journey toward unconditional love and being able to say, "I know my family and home is an emotionally safe place for everyone to be him or herself." Typically, when a teen's family and home are a safe place relationally, each person's needs are being met, no one is in distress, and there is a general feeling of calm. Then loving behaviors follow, including teens becoming more compliant and seeking connection with their parents.

As you start the journey of heart-centered parenting, you will see a change in how you view your child's behavior; instead of focusing on being enraged by such things as your teen's messy room, your teen's lack of motivation, or your teen's forgetfulness, you will begin to connect with your teen even though his room is still messy, his motivation is slowly growing, or she still forgets to do things. Your family will know how to connect in the midst of chaos. All of this occurs without focusing on and trying to control your child's behavior!

THE BEST WAY TO HELP YOUR CHILD

We believe that the best way to help your child is to help yourself. Like your teen, you have a profound desire to connect with others, including your teen. Your heart, body, and mind desire and need connection. But your connection to others is only as deep and as good as your connection with yourself. To shift your relationship with your teen (and others), you must first go inward, knowing and taking care of your feelings and needs. In the process of going inward and knowing and caring for yourself, you grow in loving yourself. You can then move outward with your true and loving self and connect with others. You then live in the moment and act from a place of love rather than the past or future, regardless of how much chaos you experience.

You are a powerful presence and influence in your child's life. In research on prevention, parents have been shown to be a key to stopping teens from engaging in drugs and alcohol.[1] And in education, decades of research show that parent involvement in their child's education is a key factor in academic success.[2] Such influence is the result of the relationship between parent and child. Heart-centered parenting will help you to take care of yourself, so you can be a powerful, loving, and influential presence in your child's life. Whatever your relationship with your child looks like now, do not underestimate how much you mean to your child, and how much you impact your child.

YOU HAVE WHAT YOU NEED

In this introduction and in the pages to follow, you will come across many new and challenging ideas, words and ways of being with yourself and your child. You are learning a new language as you learn a new way of parenting. A wonderful part of heart-centered parenting is that you already have everything you need to learn the essentials. Think about this. Feel this. While the process is challenging, *you have what you need*. And we will help you uncover it.

Keep in mind that usually, by the time a parent decides to take a heart-centered approach, relationships are rocky. So it will take time and practice to reestablish relational safety and connection with your teen. Regardless of where you are starting, you can embrace this process and take the steps to move forward.

Chaos to Connection presents nine heart-centered essentials: awareness, safety, support, presence, engagement, guidance, forgiveness, perseverance, and vision. We call these nine essentials "essential" because they are the basic and indispensable pieces of building and maintaining connections. They are natural practices that have been hidden by learned belief systems. Engaging the essentials will bring you back to your essence, deconstructing those belief systems that have prevented you from deeply connecting with yourself, your child, your family, and everyone you are in relationship with.

The essentials offer a new way to be with your feelings and emotional state, to become aware of them so that you are not unknowingly controlled by them. Your feelings are your subjective response to a person, thing, or situation. Examples of feelings are fear, pride, anger, excitement, happiness, and confusion. Emotions or your emotional state are your feelings plus physiological and behavioral changes in your body. For example, when you feel happiness, in your emotional state, your body may be relaxed. When you feel angry, your body may feel tight and clenched. We will use the words feelings and emotions or emotional state in this context throughout the book.

The essentials fall into three modes or states of being in which families function: Surviving, Reviving, and Thriving. As you move through Surviving, Reviving, and Thriving, you will never find yourself completely out of or in just one of the modes. The modes will overlap in your life even as you find yourself thriving more and more. You will continue to use and grow in all of the essentials. You will find, for example, that when you begin practicing the essentials in Surviving (awareness, safety, and support), they will take some time to establish. As you grow in these essentials, when you return to Surviving you will become more adept at using awareness, safety, and support. This will be the case in each mode—over time you become more and more adept at each essential.

What are the Surviving, Reviving, and Thriving modes in which families function? At the beginning of each section—Surviving, Reviving, and Thriving—we present a brief description of the mode, plus the characteristics and signs that indicate you are in that mode. A brief description of each mode is also presented here:

Surviving

Many of you will begin in Surviving, trying to get by day-to-day, trying to keep your heads above water, working incredibly hard to raise your kids. Family life may have deteriorated to the extent that the family is in deep distress, as if they were in the emergency room, and the situation is critical. Family life feels as intense as survival, as if someone is at risk of dying. Because of the critical situation, Surviving essentials focus on the parent and performing immediate life-saving functions.

Reviving

When families are Reviving, the parents have been stabilized, but there is much healing to be done. The healing requires loving care and learning to do things differently. As the family mends and gains strength, attention can be turned to the teen in the family and to how to change the way parents interact with their teen.

Thriving

When families are Thriving, there are gifts of time, peace, and clarity, and an absence of ongoing or regular relational crisis. The family can collectively reflect and appreciate the family members. Through forgiveness, gratitude, and play, the family becomes more tightly knit. The family has the opportunity to be strengthened and to share what they've learned with others.

When you move through the modes, you will begin to see your child from a new perspective or through a "heart lens." Though this may seem foreign now, let's take a glimpse at how a heart lens changes how parents see and interpret typical teen behavior:

FAMILY MODE	SURVIVING	REVIVING	THRIVING
	(USING THE MIND LENS)	(STARTING USING THE HEART LENS)	(USING THE HEART LENS)
What parents see:	Yelling at parent	Needing to be heard	A communication that parent needs to be present and truly listening
Interpretation:	Disrespect	Distress	A call for love
What parents see:	Refusing to do chores	Dislikes being told what to do	A communication that parents focusing more on chores than connecting
Interpretation:	Defiance	Saying no	Holding onto self
What parents see:	Couch potato	Low confidence	Need more holding of who they are
Interpretation:	Laziness	Lack of internal motivation	Needing support
What parents see:	Lying	Doing the best they can	Asking parents to take responsibility for being safe
Interpretation:	Dishonesty	Fear of getting in trouble	Needing emotional safety

We talk throughout this book about moving through Surviving, Reviving, and Thriving. These ways of functioning as a family comprise a spiral in which you continue to move upward through each mode and spending shorter amounts of time in a mode, remaining stagnant in Surviving and Reviving. Thriving happens before you know it! If you are not moving in a mode, remaining stagnant in Reviving, for example, then you will want to look at the essentials again and make adjustments. As you grow in the essentials, you will develop improved perception of where you are in this process and what you need to move.

HOW TO USE
THIS BOOK

Before we dive into the essentials, we would like to give you some tips on how to best use *Chaos to Connection* as well as lay a little language groundwork.

- *Chaos to Connection* is truly best to read in its entirety from beginning to end. The basis for using heart-centered parenting is explained in the first third of the book and is absolutely essential for grasping the later material. While the concepts are not complicated, they require a new way of thinking, and adapting takes time.

- Having said that, if you find that you are in a crisis and need immediate help, call us directly at 866-645-1781 or visit www.chaostoconnection.com. And, as always, if you or your teen are in a dangerous situation (at risk of hurting one's self or someone else), call 911.

- At the end of each chapter, there is a section on Common Challenges, describing challenges parents often experience as they move through the essentials. Though we use the phrase "Common Challenges," we want you to view your challenges as opportunities in disguise. The challenges are opportunities for you to practice heart-centered parenting. We are excited that you will continue to have challenges, because they are prime places to learn and practice the essentials.

- At the end of each chapter, you will also find Key Learnings that give a quick overview of the chapter and Personal Practices to help solidify what you have learned and to put the essentials into action.

- We as authors come from a variety of backgrounds and religious and spiritual beliefs. We created this work in a way that represents and reflects that diverse culture. *Chaos to Connection* is not associated with any one religious doctrine or spiritual belief system. At the same time, this book is not non-religious or non-spiritual, and the power of love is the common root of our beliefs. We encourage you to incorporate your beliefs into heart-centered parenting.

- The stories we use illustrate different concepts in each chapter and are based on our real-life experience.

- Throughout *Chaos to Connection*:

  * "We" refers to authors of this book, who use the essentials in the real world with individuals and family every day.

  * "Parent" refers to a parent or guardian.

  * "Family" means any number of parents or guardians and child scenarios, whether your family has one or two parents, one or more children, is headed by a grandparent or other family members, or has different- or same-sex parents.

  * We alternate between male and female in reference to your teen. In each case, we are including in the term both boys and girls.

We are excited to now dive into the heart-centered essentials, and to help you discover a new way of being with yourself and parenting your teen.

"Always we begin again."

ST. BENEDICT

I

sur·viv·ing (*verb*): remaining alive or in existence; continuing to function or prosper; being under life-threatening stress; a family functioning mode in which troubling behavior is met with reactions of fear, judgment, and shame.

Our first heart-centered essential begins in Surviving, a mode in which your family is in the emergency room fighting for survival. Your family life is characterized by chaos; your child's behavior has deteriorated to the point that you are seeking help to make your family healthier. You want the doctors to fix your child so everyone can get back home to recuperate and return to being a calm, happy family.

Families who are surviving have common characteristics. You know you're surviving if you are experiencing any or all of the following:

- High stress.
- Intense emotions and emotional reactions.
- Recurring physical reactions.
- Feeling out of control, powerless, and desperate.
- Feeling like a victim.
- Intolerance, rigidness, lack of empathy, and a black and white view of situations.
- Disconnection from physical sensations and yourself.
- Focus on teen behavior.
- Operating from your head and not your heart.

When you are Surviving, you may interpret your child's behavior in such terms as disrespectfulness, defiance, laziness, or dishonesty. Your child's behavior may also send you into an intense emotional state—raging, crying, withdrawing. The first three essentials will help you shift how you see and interpret your child's behavior and how you respond to it.

In this first section, we will define, discuss, illustrate, and help you practice the three beginning heart-centered essentials. These three essentials are Awareness, Safety, and Support.

3

AWARENESS

a·ware·ness (*noun*): mindfulness; knowing or being present with yourself; awakening to who you truly are to return to a place of love.

Much of your current efforts to improve your family's functioning likely focus on your teen; many parenting books *do* focus on the child's behavior and on controlling that behavior through consequences. You may have been taught that if you can get your teen to behave, then you can connect with them. You're probably looking for results and success in changing your child's behavior. You may want to fix your child. These are all normal feelings. That's what you've been taught. We want to show you another way.

The truth is, you are unable to control your child's behavior. Continuing to focus on your child's behavior, as we have seen, may have long-term detrimental effects on your family. What you *can* do is learn how to work with your emotions and change your own behavior, which will ultimately help your child. You can learn to be aware of yourself, to love yourself, and to return to a place of calm from which to parent your child. We describe your family as "being in the emergency room" when you are surviving. But, you are actually the patient.

We begin the nine heart-centered essentials with awareness, an essential that will strengthen you and begin to uncover your true self so that you can provide a loving presence for your child. The following story presents a typical scenario for parents who are Surviving and not yet practicing awareness:

Sarah was instantly angry when she got home and tripped over her son's skateboard in the entryway. She picked up the skateboard and yelled for her son, "James! James! Get down here right now and move this skateboard! Or I'll throw it in the trash! James!" She threw the skateboard down, narrowly missing a video game controller. She kicked the controller out of the way and stormed down the hall to James' room. She stomped on the floor hard so he would hear her coming. When Sarah got to James' door, she threw the door open and found James lying on the bed with headphones on, reading a comic book. She stormed over to him, her face contorted and hands clenched, and pulled the headphones off his ears. "James! Didn't you hear me! Your skateboard! Again! If you can't figure out a way to put it away when you're done with it, I'm going to throw it in the trash!" Sarah stormed back out of the room, slamming James' bedroom door behind her.

Let's look now at ways to develop awareness, and we'll return to this story at the end of the chapter to illustrate the change awareness brings.

Heart-centered parenting begins with mindfulness. By mindfulness we mean developing awareness about yourself, turning your attention to what you are feeling physically and emotionally, and to what you are thinking. Throughout a regular day, we receive a lot of sensory information or stimuli —sounds, sights, smells, touches. Fortunately, for most of us, our bodies are so designed that we can quickly sense, interpret, and choose whether to ignore or react to information. As you are reading this book, you are likely ignoring the feel of the chair you are sitting on, the smell of the air, and sounds around you. Scientists refer to this as "sensory integration," the ability to filter in the relevant information while simultaneously filtering out the irrelevant. We can and do ignore, to varying degrees, a lot of the information we receive.[1] Sensory integration is necessary to our being able to function and can be a challenge for those who are unable to integrate well.

However, we become so proficient at filtering information that we also filter out important information from our own bodies—fatigue, hunger, pain—and our feelings and thoughts. When you filter too much, you miss key communication! So much of the time, we adults tend to see the world from our mind, viewing the world according to logic, thoughts, and beliefs we have come to accept. We filter out or reject messages from our body and heart. In this way, we live above the surface, progressively losing sight of our body and heart.

Some stress—productive stress—is good for us, helping to motivate and energize and even being beneficial to our health.[2] But intense and ongoing stress, as you experience in Surviving, is not good for us for a variety of reasons. In times of intense momentary and prolonged stress, you filter out even more as we go into fight-or-flight[3] mode. Our body engages every bodily function and ability toward responding to the danger of the situation, including our thinking. Because thinking and choosing a response take time, and time is of the essence in a dangerous situation, thinking and choosing are turned off in favor of an instinctual response.[4] While this is a good response for surviving, it gets in the way of truly thriving and connecting to those around us.

When you are Surviving, due to stress, your body and mind are responding as if your life is in danger. Let's take a step back from Surviving. Remind yourself that you are not truly in danger for your life. Life is chaotic, but you are going to live. Give your body the opportunity to stop engaging in Surviving and to start engaging in awareness.

Rather than filtering out information, in awareness you practice being intensely aware of information, of what you are feeling physically and emotionally as well as what you are thinking. You go below the surface of what your mind says. Rather than being mindless, on auto pilot, you become mindful. We have found that awareness or mindfulness is essential to parents connecting to their children. Indeed, research has shown that mindfulness has incredible impact on us and our relationships,[5] including improving our relationships with friends and family,[6] improving how we handle stress,[7] strengthening our immune system,[8] and increasing empathy.[9] True awareness lives in the present moment—lives in sensing rather than filtering information. Two ways to become more aware are through self-care and curiosity, which we explore next.

SELF-CARE

As you become mindful and grow your self-awareness, you will recognize the need to take care of yourself. You are the foundation of love and leadership in your family, and being effective at this requires knowing and taking care of yourself. We often hear from parents, "But I've been taught that a parent should be selfless, without any human needs or wants." Indeed, by caring for yourself you are not being selfish but developing self-love. You can't be the best parent possible if you don't take care of yourself.

Self-care is a natural step in awareness, because your awareness will help you to reduce your stress and literally help you to take care of your body. Ongoing stress and constant stress reactions are linked to compromised immune systems, high blood pressure, depression, skin problems, headaches, back pain, insomnia, digestive disorders, heart disease, and stroke.[10] For these reasons, we encourage you to take care of yourself—your heart, body, and mind. Whatever is happening with your child, you need to take time and energy now to take care of yourself. When you are able to interact with your child from an emotionally aware and physically healthy place, you will be able to offer a new level of love and new way of parenting to your child. You may find as you take care of yourself that you notice new things—feelings, beliefs, interests—that have been there but haven't had time to surface. You will find more opportunities to love all of you.

You can improve your health and outlook considerably by just taking a little time to catch up on exercise, nutrition, and rest. A wellness check like the one below done every day (or several times a day) can help you remember to be aware of your body. You might sit down and close your eyes for five minutes, slowly getting feedback from every part of your body. Or you might grab a bottle of water and walk around the block. The most important thing is to get outside of your mind by focusing on your body.

Wellness Check

Scan your body and take care of its needs using the following prompts:

+ Are my shoulders hunched, or are other body parts "clenched"? (relax, stretch)
+ How's my breathing? (take deep, cleansing breaths)
+ Am I thirsty? (drink water)
+ Am I hungry or overfull? (eat smart, drink water)
+ Am I tired? (change bedtime routine, nap, relax)
+ Do I need to interact with someone? (interact)
+ Do I need to be alone? (take time to be alone)

As you take care of yourself, you will start to feel better and to recognize that your child's behavior is not a reflection on you. You will start to separate your child's behavior from you. You will also start to fill up internally and have greater capacity to be loving with your child. Love cannot come from emptiness. Take time every day to check in with yourself and to care for yourself.

Curiosity is a powerful way to think of awareness about yourself. If you are curious about yourself, you're not judging or shaming but moving in and opening up, exploring yourself, your experience, and your heart. Being curious doesn't have an expectation of an outcome.

Consider curiosity in another way, as a heart lens. Much of the time, we see the world from our mind lens, making sense of the world according to what our mind says. Our mind lens uses what we've been taught and what we've come to believe. Often the mind lens feels stiff, strict, and judgmental. For example, when your mind lens sees your teen yelling at you, your mind lens interprets the behavior as disrespect. This interpretation comes from what you've been taught or come to believe, such as, this is not what respectful teens do, or that as a child you were not respected when your parents yelled. A heart lens, on the other hand, sees below the surface of the mind's interpretation and feels open, loving, and compassionate. Your heart lens sees that your child needs love when he yells and accepts the yelling for what it is. As you are curious about yourself, turn your heart lens on yourself, and view yourself with openness, love, and compassion.

To become curious about yourself, start by being present with your body. Scan your body now and the next time you are in a tense moment. You might use such questions as, "What is the physical feeling in my body when I'm upset? Where do I feel that physically in my body?" These sensations might include tightness or pain in your shoulders, a tightness or heaviness in your chest, feeling like you got punched in the stomach, clenching your hands or toes, a complete absence of feeling or sensations in your body, or a rush of energy.

Become curious about what your body is sensing by touch, smell, hearing, and sight, now and in a tense moment. Tune into external sensations. As you are curious about your body, your mind will have thoughts. Be present to these. You will have feelings. Be present to these. Be curious about the feelings that you have. Tune into internal feelings. Name them.

Your curiosity about yourself focuses your awareness on you and develops your heart lens, so that you see below your surface and listen to the messages of your body and heart. Awareness will start to give you a sense of openness and will open a way to openness for your teen. As you practice mindfulness, you show your teen a new way. Awareness can penetrate into the whole family. Let's look again at the story from the beginning of the chapter with your new understanding of awareness:

Sarah was instantly angry when she got home and tripped over her son's skateboard in the entryway. She felt her blood pressure rising. She was about to react and yell for her son. Instead, she stopped, took a breath and just felt the anger inside her. The discomfort was palpable. She felt a rush of energy and tightness in her chest, but instead of throwing her anger out toward her son, she took the time to feel her anger inside. Sarah didn't try to shift the feeling down or to act it out, she just felt the amazing power of her anger. Seeing how big the charge was, she became clear that this was bigger than a skateboard. Sarah sat with it and breathed.

In our work with families, we have found that parents have common challenges to learning and practicing awareness. Some of these include how to give yourself time and space to grow your awareness, when only one parent in a two-parent household is interested in learning about heart-centered parenting, when a parent is held back by self-blame, or when a parent is hesitant to focus on himself because he feels selfish.

You may find that your response to your teen's behavior presents a challenge to being curious about yourself. To be mindful and curious, you will need to give yourself time and space. You will need to relax into awareness. Remember that you don't have to respond to your teen right now—and not responding is a good idea because you're in a high state of stress. If you have to take yourself

11

physically out of the moment with your child, do so. You can use such phrases as the following with your child:

- "Can we talk about this later?"
- "I'm sorry, that scares me. Please wait. I need to sit with this for a while."
- "I'm sorry, I shouldn't have said that. Let's have a 'do over' later."
- "I'm too angry to talk about this now."
- "Wait, let's start over."
- "Please try to think about this from my point of view. Let's set a time to talk about this again."

Then find a safe place to be with yourself and breathe. Remember also that your child's behavior is really her best attempt to meet her needs.

You may be beginning the journey of heart-centered parenting without your spouse or partner wanting to join you. In these situations, we've noticed that often when one parent starts heart-centered parenting, the other parent follows. In a family with a mother and father, for instance, the mother starts practicing awareness before the father. As the mother gets better and better at awareness and her connection with her child begins to change, the father gets curious and starts asking about what the mother is doing. The father eventually asks, "OK, what is this?", providing a time for the mother to share about awareness. If this is a challenge for you, continue practicing and notice how your partner becomes curious.

We have put the focus of this chapter on parents and on parents taking responsibility for their behavior and actions toward their children. As some parents work on becoming self-aware, they face the challenge of being held back by self-blame, blaming themselves for their child's behavior, and thinking of themselves as a "bad parent." While the focus right now is you, this is not because you are a bad person or a bad parent, but because you are no longer able to help others until you become self-aware and regain strength. You are the focus because the solution lies within you. You may not feel this is true, or you may feel shame and blame. These are important feelings to surface and work through. If you continue to focus on your child while you are highly stressed, your ability to help your child decreases considerably. Keep in mind that you and your child are not broken. Your relationship is broken.

Finally, many parents feel hesitant to begin working on themselves because it feels selfish. Such work requires you to take your focus off your child and possibly others in your family. It is important to keep in mind that in this state, you cannot change the apparent cause of all this stress—your child's behavior.

Asking parents to stop focusing on the teen and start focusing on themselves is the hardest thing we practitioners do. Parents naturally react against it. But if you're a parent struggling with a teen, you need to suspend that natural instinct for a while. Here are a few things to remember:

- This is not "selfish." Remember that the family is an ecosystem. Making you healthier is the first step in making the family healthier.
- Taking care of yourself is a beginning piece of an overall process of deepening relationships. *Chaos to Connection* will continue to help you learn to engage productively and lovingly with your teen.
- If the teen-first instinct is especially strong in you, that's a good thing. That burning desire to help your child can be channeled in lots of productive ways. For one thing, it may help you stay focused on this difficult journey to heart-centered parenting. You can divert some of that energy to taking care of yourself, especially in the early stages of learning heart-centered parenting. Though it may be difficult for your son or daughter to admit, you are the foundation on which he or she absolutely depends. That foundation needs an ongoing check-up, care, and maintenance.

- You are not able to control your child's feelings or behavior. You *are* able to take responsibility for your feelings and behavior.
- Mindfulness means turning your attention to what you are feeling physically and emotionally and to what you are thinking.
- You can use self-care to anchor yourself in the present moment and to grow awareness of yourself.
- Getting curious about yourself will help develop a heart lens and your awareness.

1. As a practice today, name as many moments as possible. Such as, "I am walking to my car. I am tense. I am talking with my child. I am driving down the road. My eyes are tired. I smell smoke in the air," etc. In just naming the action you are engaged in, you will become more present. We are so often in our thoughts more than paying attention to our present moment.

2. Get to know yourself by identifying how you respond to stress. Ask yourself which of these common stress reactions you have:

Physical Sensations	*Emotional Sensations*
Change in eating habits	Abrupt changes in mood or personality
Nausea	Anxiousness
Drug, alcohol abuse	Intolerance
Shallow breathing or shortness of breath	Apathy
Shoulders high (neck and shoulder tension)	Lack of pleasure in what you used to enjoy
Sleep disturbances	Distractedness
Tightness in throat, diaphragm	Poor concentration, decision-making
Listlessness	Repetitive, negative thinking
Displays of aggression	Extreme or prolonged bouts of emotion
(punching, throwing things, etc.)	Extreme irritability
Insomnia	Feelings of desperation
Demanding, controlling behavior	Forgetfulness
Simple tasks feel like a chore	Impatience

3. Use a guided meditation to practice awareness, such as one of the following:
   Three-Minute Meditation[12]

- In a quiet room, stand, sit, or lie down on a soft surface.
- Close your eyes.
- For a minute or so, scan your body and notice what's happening. Notice any feelings of heaviness or tightness. Notice any movements you are making.

- For another minute, breathe slowly and deeply. As you exhale, remember that you're not doing or trying to change anything. Just let your various thoughts drift through your mind.
- Listen to the sounds around you. Just listen without identifying the sounds. Notice any silences between the sounds. Again, notice how your body feels.
- Slowly open your eyes.

3-2-1 Meditation [13]

In a quiet room, stand, sit, or lie down on soft surface.
- State in a calm and slow voice, "Now I am aware of **seeing**" and slowly name **three** things you see.
- Take three deep breaths through your nose.
- State in a calm and slow voice, "Now I am aware of **hearing**" and slowly name **three** things you hear.
- Take three deep breaths through your nose.
- State in a calm and slow voice, "Now I am aware of **feeling** in my body" and slowly name **three** sensations that you feel on or inside your body.
- Take three deep breaths through your nose.
- State in a calm and slow voice, "Now I am aware of **seeing**" and slowly state **two** things you are seeing.
- Take three deep breaths through your nose.
- State in a calm and slow voice, "Now I am aware of **hearing**" and slowly name **two** things you hear.
- Take three deep breaths through your nose.
- State in a calm and slow voice, "Now I am aware of **feeling** in my body" and slowly name **two** sensations that you feel on or inside your body.
- Take three deep breaths through your nose.
- State in a calm and slow voice, "Now I am aware of **seeing**" and slowly state **one** thing you are seeing.
- Take three deep breaths through your nose.
- State in a calm and slow voice, "Now I am aware of **hearing**" and slowly name **one** thing you hear.
- Take three deep breaths through your nose.
- State in a calm and slow voice, "Now I am aware of **feeling** in my body" and slowly name **one** sensation that you feel on or inside your body.
- Take three deep breaths through your nose.

"The only real voyage of discovery consists not in seeking new landscapes but in having new eyes."

MARCEL PROUST

2

SAFETY

safe·ty *(noun):* the state of not being exposed to danger; security, asylum, and refuge; a state in your family in which each person has space for his own feelings and essential self.

You have done some work up to this point on mindfulness, becoming more aware of your heart and body so that you can be ready to help your teen. In this chapter, you will begin to see how the work you have done leads you to providing relational and emotional safety for your family, an essential part of moving from chaos to connection.

Relational safety is providing the kind of relationship in which you and others can interact freely and with love in all the aspects of a relationship. When there is relational safety, those in the relationship flourish. In order to have relational safety with another person, you have to have emotional safety, which we will discuss next.

EMOTIONAL SAFETY

As a parent, you play many roles—caregiver, advisor, chauffeur, chef, bank, asylum, and guardian. All of these roles have a common theme, being a loving leader. By loving leader we mean a parent who shows a child the way with unconditional love.

When a family has emotional safety, any member of the family has the space to express his or her own experiences and feelings, whether those might be judged by some as good or bad or "too big." A family member's experiences or emotions are not met with resistance or a desire for change but rather with love, exactly where he or she is at the moment. Whatever any member of the family experiences, when there is emotional safety, each family member knows that at home he or she will find love, compassion, space to have needs met, and understanding. The family members reflect each person's innate loveability and self-worth, and each member is seen, heard, and validated. To be loved and accepted at our worst is the gift of unconditional love. It is this love which ultimately helps us to connect with our authentic self.

As an example, read the following story about a mom and her son:

Jeff was recovering from problems with drugs and alcohol, and he struggled with a lot of anxiety and stress. He tended to become very controlling over his mom, Melanie, bullying her and telling her what to do. Melanie was concerned about not doing anything that would trigger Jeff and cause him to regress, to feel rejected, and to eventually abuse drugs and alcohol again. Melanie bought Jeff a car with the agreement that he would mow the lawn to pay her back, something she needed help with because of her health. Soon, Jeff let the grass grow wild. Melanie started fuming. Without telling Jeff, she sold the car. When Jeff found out about his car being sold, he yelled at his mom and started bullying her even more.

This story may be familiar. As may be the parent's response and the feeling in the home—high stress, worry on the part of the parents, the parents feeling like they can't do anything to make the situation better and responding to the teen with consequences. This scenario creates an emotionally unsafe home where no one can express his or her struggles or joys. However, you can create different results in similar situations by developing emotional safety. We'll show you how.

TRIGGERS

The first step in providing emotional safety is learning to recognize your triggers. Since you, the parent, are the patient here, let's look at what your teen's behavior does to you. When your teen acts out through anger, drug use, defiance, disconnection, sexual promiscuity, lack of motivation, or spending lots of time playing video games or on the computer, you have a reaction—probably a strong one. We call this reaction "being triggered," and those behaviors or actions on the part of your teen that initiate your reaction, "triggers."

When you are triggered, you have a rush of emotion, a rush so strong that you believe it to be true. You are truly angry at your teen! Your teen is truly misbehaving! Your teen will truly end up a failure! But your trigger is misleading. It takes you away from awareness and prevents you from seeing what is really going on. Your trigger's only mission is to act out and to control your child.

Your trigger is misleading in two ways. Your trigger is not who you truly are, and what it wants—to control your child—will not make you feel better. Triggers happen in times of stress, a time when our logical brain cannot engage. Because your body follows a prescribed sequence as soon as stress or danger is perceived and a cascade of hormones send you into "fight-or-flight" mode,[1] you cannot think clearly. In this survival mode, your mind is more childish than adult, and the higher functions of your brain—planning, reasoning—are not engaged. You can learn how to *act* rather than *react* to your triggers in times of stress.[2] This is as simple as starting by naming your trigger and immediately stepping away from it.

Triggers are signs of deep emotions being stirred up. And by drawing your awareness to the triggers, turning your heart lens on them, the feeling will release itself. You can then begin to discover beliefs and messages, often manifested as particular sensitivities, associated with those feelings from past experiences. In our work with families, feelings of fear, shame, and judgment typically create triggers. Parents may fear that ten years down the road their teen will be irresponsible, disrespectful, not be contributing members of society, waste their life away, never develop a work ethic, drop out of school, not go to college, go to jail, or be violent if they continue acting as they are acting. Parents may feel ashamed that their child is acting the way he is. Parents may place judgment on their child—she's lazy and entitled—or on themselves, thinking, "I'm such a bad parent" or "What will my friends think of her and me?" Such future thinking wraps a belief around your feeling, hiding the truth behind the feeling. Beneath your trigger is a world of feeling for you to explore.

You are solely responsible for your emotions. Your trigger might tell you otherwise. When you are triggered by your teen's behavior and you react by trying to control your teen's behavior through consequences (grounding, taking away a car or money, taking away a privilege or something the teen enjoys), you are placing the responsibility for how you feel on your teen. When you are triggered, you feel uncomfortable and want to take action to remove the discomfort. You may try to control your teen so that you can feel better. In essence, when you do this, you are sending the unspoken message to your teen, "If you would behave in a way that I want you to, then I would be okay." But the problem with this is that your teen doesn't need or want to take care of you. Furthermore, put yourself in your teen's shoes. Is she going to want to move towards you when you are in this emotional state? Always, always, each person is responsible for her own emotions.

Your trigger—as strong and real as it seems—is an obstacle. When you are triggered and communicate based on that trigger, your interaction with your teen escalates. You may get angry, then your teen gets angry and you build on each other's anger. Your trigger connects with your teen rather than you. Further, if you continue to allow your trigger to motivate your reactions, your teen will never get to connect with you, your true self, and all the emotions that underlie your trigger. You will be unable to connect with your child in such a state. Your teen will be unable to share her true self with you because your trigger prevents such sharing.

You can start to move from Surviving by growing your awareness of the emotions and needs underlying your triggers. As you continue in this chapter, you will find your awareness growing through the following process:

Teen's Behavior or Action ➤ Your Trigger ➤ Grace Gap: Stop, Sit, Breathe ➤ Emotional Cycle

Let's look now at the next step, the Grace Gap.

THE GRACE GAP

You are a wonderful, mysterious, and magnificent creature. Here you are, in an intense, chaotic family situation, and your mind is doing the best it can to help you and your family survive. Remember that you are not in a true life or death situation, even though your mind convinces you otherwise and even though you feel otherwise.

Triggers are part of life. They will never completely go away. Nor will the fear, shame, and judgment that are part of them. You can, however, start reacting differently to your triggers. As psychiatrist and holocaust survivor Viktor Frankl observed, "Between stimulus and response there is a space. In that space is our power to choose our response. In our response lies our growth and our freedom."[3] Your task when you are triggered is to pull out of your trigger and to practice awareness to come into the present moment. Just stop. If you feel your guns coming out, shove them back in the holster. Your trigger wants nothing more than to act out. It is as if you regress to being a toddler, and you just want your way!

As an example of what to do with a trigger, consider a father who is angry about his son's grades and the notification from the school that he may not graduate. Rather than reacting to the news, the father notices his strong feeling, sits down, and just feels his anger. He names it, "I am angry." In stopping your trigger, you create what we call a Grace Gap, a space between your trigger and your reaction in which you can choose your reaction. To create a Grace Gap, remember the following: stop talking, sit down, and breathe. Stop, Sit, and Breathe.

We call this space a Grace Gap because you extend grace to yourself (and your child), a space of kindness and pardon in an intense moment. In this space, you are loving yourself by stepping back from your trigger's desired action and using your awareness.

In the Grace Gap, you act to anchor yourself in the present moment, rather than in your trigger, by bringing awareness to your present-moment experiences. For example, a parent who finds marijuana in her child's room—an experience that can certainly trigger a parent—can name the present moment to become aware, "There is a bag of marijuana on Joe's bed. I am holding a bag of marijuana that was on Joe's bed. The marijuana is brown and green. I feel a tightness in my chest and my toes are curled." Again, stating the facts of a situation to yourself can bring you into the moment.

Additionally, as you become familiar with the physical sensations triggers activate, memorize the physical sensation (i.e., clenching, a rush of energy, or complete absence of feeling sensations in your body) and use this sensation as a clue that you are being triggered and as a clue to pull into the present moment. Often if we are not paying attention to our emotions, they come out in physical feelings or pain.

In the Grace Gap, you draw yourself into the present moment through awareness rather than quickly discharging your trigger. Once you are in the present moment, you have the space to go through what we call an "emotional cycle," in which you uncover what is beneath your trigger and return to a place of calm.

Now you may be wondering as you become aware of your emotions what to do with them. The emotional cycle provides a helpful description of how to work with your emotions. In the emotional cycle, a point of stress, such as your child's behavior, enters your world and triggers you. You can choose to get off the emotional cycle by directing your emotions at your child and trying to control her behavior. Or you can use what you know about awareness to follow the cycle, being curious about your feelings and really feeling it, following your feelings all the way back to a place of calm, strength, and love. When you choose to shortchange the cycle, you shortchange your self, your emotional growth, and your relationship with your child. When you complete the cycle, you have a better understanding of your self, you have taken responsibility for your own emotional state, and you return to a place of calm and love.

To help you grasp the concept of the emotional cycle, consider the following analogy. On river rafting trips, guides instruct riders on what to do if they fall off the raft and into a sink hole. The riders are to curl up into a ball, surrender, and allow the river to take them to the bottom. In this position, the river will spit the person out. The challenge for the person is to surrender and not struggle to get to the top, which is the initial instinct. This is exactly what is required when sitting with intense emotions. When we feel our discomfort, in relation to our children's behavior, we fall into a hole. We struggle to pop ourselves out of the emotional hole, resisting and doing everything we can, including giving our teen consequences and controlling and shaming the behavior. But the necessary work is to curl into that ball and surrender as you allow the emotions to take you to the bottom of the hole, and then pop you back out. Instead of struggling to control the behavior or trying to get your child to rescue you, you must go to the bottom of the hole and penetrate the belief that creates the intense emotion.

Steps in Emotional Cycle
1. A behavior or action triggers you.
2. Feelings arise with beliefs from the past.
3. Belief intensifies the feelings.
4. Grace Gap - Stop!

5. Sit and breathe with the feelings, telling the truth, "These are just feelings," "I will be OK," "These feelings will not kill me," "This is just a belief, it is not real."

6. Really feel the feelings until the truth about your need is revealed.

7. Let that part of you that has a need know you will take care of it.

8. Feelings dissipate, you feel calm and loved.

Early on, surrendering to the river and getting to a calm and loving place may take a while. You'll find that it's sometimes impractical to avoid your teen altogether while you calm yourself, expand awareness, and get to the root cause of your emotional reaction. So you might try to interact in a loving way over minor issues. It's also possible that you feel too angry with your teen to interact at all. That may be okay. Chances are, she wants some space too. You'll find a balance.

Let's look at the following story in which a dad completes an emotional cycle:

When Mike came home after a long day at work, the first thing he saw was a messy living room with books, shoes, dishes, video games, and food wrappers on the floor and couch. He felt angry finding his house and the couch where he wanted to relax in such disarray. The anger felt big, and he had the urge to walk through the living room, kicking everything around, and breaking things on the floor. But instead of acting out his anger, he felt the anger and the power. Seeing how big the anger was, Mike realized the feeling had more to it than the messy room. Mike stopped, sat, and breathed.

Mike took a moment to tell the truth about that bigger part. He was able to see his huge feelings were more connected to what the mess symbolized; namely, not being appreciated and valued. He had asked his kids countless times to clean up the living room when they were done, and when they left a mess one more time, under stress he regressed to a younger age. He felt inside his own helplessness and fear. He saw his belief rise up that he would never have a good enough job to be valued.

Seeing the situation through that belief made him responsible for taking care of himself and validating his own worth. His kids couldn't do that for him! Mike had to do it for himself, and he did. In that space, he opened up to seeing his kids as the kids that they were and recognized that they still needed him to be the adult who could help them remember to clean up. This was really just a messy living room, not a personal attack. In his moment of anger, he chose not to give all his power to his kids and their actions.

When you have a strong feeling, really be present with your feeling—let the anger or sadness or fear rise and come out. Have acceptance for your feeling. You might cry. You might be afraid of being overwhelmed by the feeling. Your natural response is fight or flight, to find a way to remove the pain. But sit with the feeling. Let it rise and crest, and you will then feel it recede. Your feelings are only feelings. You are not your feelings, nor will you become your feelings. Imagine giving your feelings—that tidal wave of fear, anger, or sadness—a hug. Take the step to love the feeling for what it is and what it has done for you. Discover how you can move from feeling intense, painful feeling to feeling less emotional. It may help to take a walk, talk to a friend, cry, sit quietly, meditate, pray, go for a drive, or take a bath. Find out what helps you take care of you.

One of the most dramatic changes that happens when you grow in awareness and complete the emotional cycle is that you express honest rather than triggered emotions with your child. She begins to see that you are a safe person to approach and that you value honest feelings. If you struggle with anger toward your child, for instance, you give him the message that, "I am not safe for you." Your anger can be really scary for your child, and he will react with more anger. Instead, stop, sit, breathe, and be with your anger. You can contain it, hold it, and release it. You can then come back to meet your child and accept him where he is.

When you have created this emotional safety for yourself, you are in a place where you can offer emotional safety. Remember, emotional safety is accepting your child exactly where he or she is. You are in a place where if chaos happens again, you can move to connection. If your child fails a class again, smokes pot again, disrespects you again, yells at you again, steals money from you again, you can express your emotions and needs, fulfill your own needs, and give room to your teen to express her emotions and needs.

Did you know you were making so many changes in how you relate to your child? Already! By moving closer to yourself, you are moving closer to your child. Your child senses the change when you take care of yourself and may want to move toward you, too.

We will talk about this in more depth in Chapter 5: Engagement, but it is good to remember that part of being with your teen in a loving way is living together in a way that everyone's needs are met. There will doubtless be times when you and your teen's needs are at odds (i.e., you need to get a good night's sleep, and your teen needs to be up late; or you need to take some time for awareness and self-care, and your teen needs you right now). You will need to balance how such competing needs get met and, at times, set boundaries.

"Boundary" has become a popular term in modern-day relationships and has been used in a variety of ways. In the context of parenting, boundaries are often seen as rules enforced in the home. Boundaries as rules are used to control a child and actually keep parents from connecting with their child. We encourage you to reset how you think of boundaries from set rules to internal or external actions you take to keep your integrity and avoid sacrificing yourself. Such boundaries are changeable, according to what you need. Your internal boundaries address your needs but still allow a door for your child to connect with you.

Whenever you have the urge to set a boundary, ask yourself why you want to set the boundary. If you are setting a "boundary" to control your child based on your fear (she'll get hurt), shame (what will the neighbors think?), or judgment (her behavior is just not right), you are not setting a boundary but a rule to control your child. If you are setting a boundary because you have a true need (for sleep, to take care of yourself, to have the grass mowed, to not give your son money to buy drugs), then you are setting a healthy boundary. Setting healthy boundaries requires you to discover your own feelings and needs. A rule, in contrast, allows you to skip over self-awareness and to go straight to relying on rules to manage your emotions. Neither you nor your child benefits from rules. Your child may follow the rules or fight against them, both at the expense of an authentic relationship.

Healthy boundaries will help you take care of your needs and create emotional safety, because you are not controlling your child and asking her to take care of your needs. When you set a boundary, your child may not like it, and you will need to give her space to have her feeling about it. For an example of resetting boundaries, let's take a look at the following story:

Dana and Mark set a curfew for their daughter Michelle, choosing a time they thought was reasonable. Night after night, Michelle came home after curfew with excuses about her friends needing her help or forgetting her watch. Night after night, Dana and Mark met her at the door and told her that they couldn't trust her. When this approach didn't work, they tried grounding her, taking away her car keys and her cell phone. Yet, Michelle continued to fight against her curfew.

Dana and Mark defended their actions as being good parents and setting strong boundaries because Michelle needed them, no matter how hard she fought. Michelle's fighting against the curfew became the focus of Michelle and her parents' relationship. The power struggle continued as the relationship continued to deteriorate.

When Dana and Mark checked in with themselves as to why they set a curfew, they got clear that they wanted Michelle to get a good night's rest, and became even more clear that they needed a good night's rest. They were also worried about Michelle's safety if she didn't come home at a reasonable hour. Not knowing where she was or what she was doing made them feel powerless, creating a need to control her actions. Dana and Mark discovered that they set a boundary out of fear instead of setting an internal boundary addressing their needs and attending to them while still attending to Michelle's needs.

When they discovered this, Dana and Mark sat down with Michelle, in a loving way, and expressed their needs and how they were going to take care of them, instead of making her responsible for them. Through being open and honoring the relationship, they were all able to agree on a time that worked for everyone. On nights when Michelle was out and they began to feel anxious, Dana and Mark decided to reach out and check in with Michelle through a text.

Dana and Mark started to recognize that they were being triggered by their daughter's late nights. They discovered the underlying emotions and motivations behind the curfew and reset their rule to a boundary, taking care of their own needs rather than acting out of fear. When you are honest about your own emotions and needs, your teen then has the room to express herself and her needs rather than reacting to rules you design.

EMOTIONAL CYCLE FOR YOUR TEEN

You may be wondering how all of this helps your child. Above, we described the emotional cycle for you and resetting boundaries to make your home emotionally safe. When your child has emotional safety at home, he has the safety and space he needs to move through this same emotional cycle, providing him with the ability to find love and self-soothe. By contrast, if you stop your child's emotional cycle by placating your child or shutting her down, you shortchange your child and your child's relationship with you.

When teens have emotional safety and the space to move through an emotional cycle, they begin to learn that feelings are just indicators of needs. They learn that even though the need may not be met by their parents, their feelings will still be seen, heard, and validated. They stop looking to external things to stop the intense feelings, and they begin to tolerate the intensity and to allow themselves to complete the cycle. Once the teen's emotional state dissipates, they can then find ways to meet those needs inside themselves or let them go. By giving your teen emotional safety in which to have full emotional cycles, you help your teen create a new neural pattern in which strong feeling is moved through internally rather than diverted to something external.

As an example, a father finds out his teen had sex for the first time and feels angry. If the father chooses to act out his anger on his teen, yelling or giving consequences, he derails himself from the emotional cycle and from getting to a place where he can be emotionally safe for his teen. His trigger meets his teen. As the father derails himself, he also derails his teen, who may be on his own emotional cycle. The teen gets stuck at the place he is when his father gets angry and intervened, and rather than being able to share his experience and emotions, he stops the emotions and finds another way to soothe himself—possibly violence, drugs, more sex, withdrawing, or going to his friends.

In contrast, if the father completes his emotional cycle—however much time and self-care he needs to do this—he does not derail himself or his teen. His teen, having the space and example from his father, is able to complete the emotional cycle, feel everything he needs to feel, and return to a place of calm and love. When a parent sits in the discomfort of a high-stress moment and feels everything, the child has the space to feel everything and learns he can get back to love by just moving through the feeling, rather than finding external soothers.

As you've learned, heart-centered parenting is not about controlling behavior but about facing intense emotions yourself and modeling that behavior for your teen. Your child needs to learn how to navigate through her own fear and discomfort by finding love and compassion within herself. Punishment and consequences cannot address these deeper needs. Let's look at the story from the beginning of the chapter about Melanie and Jeff, the car Melanie bought and the lawn Jeff hasn't mowed. This time, the grass has started to grow wild again, but Melanie takes a different approach by being emotionally safe, helping herself, and opening the door to Jeff helping himself.

Melanie started fuming, and she wanted to punish Jeff by just selling the car. Recognizing that she had been triggered and using awareness skills, Melanie looked at why she was reacting so strongly and what her needs were. She discovered she was triggered by what she saw as laziness and disrespect. She also thought about what boundaries she needed. She came to know that what she needed was to take care of herself and to get help with the yard. Melanie developed a natural consequence, rather than a punishment. She decided to use car payment money to pay someone to mow her yard and gave Jeff the responsibility for the car payment

When Melanie told Jeff about his responsibility for the payment, she was at a place where she could empathize with Jeff and say, "Jeff, I'm sorry you allowed that to happen. I really am. But I had to take care of what was important to me." Melanie's self-disclosure opened the door to Jeff explaining why he had not mowed the yard. It turned out that Jeff didn't like where his mom had moved, a less affluent neighborhood. He felt a lot of anxiety, fear, and shame because of the living situation, so he was resisting being there and helping her take care of the house and yard. Both Jeff and Melanie felt a shift in their relationship due to Melanie's self-love and self-care. In the long term, Jeff started showing Melanie more respect.

Melanie's actions and decisions led her to creating emotional safety in her relationship with Jeff, opening up a place where she shared her needs and feelings with him, and he could do the same.

COMMON CHALLENGES

Connecting to safety, as we define it, can be frightening as you let go of controlling your child and focus on your emotional safety. Emotions in your life will be high! You may have some of the following common challenges: feeling as if you are rewarding your child's behavior, fear about keeping your child safe, hesitation about the steps to emotional safety, and concerns for other children in your family.

In creating emotional safety, do you believe you are allowing your child to get away with her behavior? In the past, you did something to stop the behavior, but now you are no longer addressing that behavior through threats or consequences. The short answer is, no, you are not rewarding or accepting your child's behavior. It may help to realize that your child's behavior is partly due to the unsafe emotional environment in the home. You are not rewarding the bad behavior, but addressing a cause of it by increasing the safety of your home. You are making the change from withdrawing love when your child acts out to always being there for her, in whatever state she is in.

If you are worried about your child's physical safety—she'll be hurt or die living on the streets, doing drugs, drinking and driving, he'll get his girlfriend pregnant or get a sexually transmitted infection— you will struggle to provide emotional safety. A step for you, if you are worried about your teen's safety, is to step back and use discernment and awareness about the situation. We find that often when a teen engages in risky behavior, the teen has taken the precautions they need to keep themselves safe. How real is the threat to your teen? Can you find a way to check on her safety without removing her from it? Use your awareness to get clear about your fears and the reality of your teen's safety. Parents who move in and pull their teen out of a situation that they perceive as dangerous without attuning and listening to their teen (two topics we'll cover in Chapter 4: Presence and Chapter 5: Engagement) can lead to a major break in the relational safety. Sitting with and embracing the truth that you can't ultimately keep your teen safe allows you to move toward what you can do in the moment, which is to offer love and to create emotional safety. In the end, emotional safety is the only way to create physical safety.

When parents are working on creating emotional safety, some parents hesitate at doing the emotional work. The suggestion of diving into your feelings and sitting with the whole BIG feeling is scary! BIG feelings can seem like they are never going to end and like they will literally overwhelm you. You might struggle to find the time to work with your emotions, or you may just want to escape. You may be afraid of what working with your emotions will uncover, what they will require of you, and how relationships will shift. This is the power of feelings, but not the reality. We want to remind you that yes, you have what you need, and yes, you must work with your feelings. Remember that feelings are only feelings, and you are not your feelings. Feelings and this challenge of working with your emotions are a gift to bring you closer to yourself and your child. If you really feel your feelings and complete the emotional cycle, you will return to a place of calm and love. It may be helpful to you to have a support person with you as you go through an emotional cycle. If you are in a situation where you feel like you can be supported by a friend, and you feel the emotions rising, let yourself feel them and go through the emotional cycle with that friend.

Additionally, when your child has her BIG feeling, it may trigger your BIG feelings, and you begin to feel discomfort. Instead of allowing the feeling to dissipate and your child to return to a place of calm on his own, you may stop your child's emotional cycle because of your own discomfort. Remember the importance of your child completing the emotional cycle and that the BIG feelings are only feelings. Given your support, your child will return to calm and will grow in her ability to handle intense feelings in the future. Consider also that there is so much happening for your teen that you may not know what your teen needs, and you don't want to stop your child's feelings based on your assumptions.

We recognize that while much of the focus of *Chaos to Connection* is on you and your teen, you may have other children in your family. If this is the case, you may have additional challenges to creating safety in your home. We often see two typical scenarios in a family with multiple children and with a teen who is acting out, stemming from the parents' judgment. In one scenario, the teen who is acting out is labeled the "aggressor" and another child is labeled the "victim." In the other scenario, the children are labeled "bad" and "good." The children receive their attention according to their label—for being aggressive, for being a victim, for being bad or being good. The children become opposed to each other because their role and the way they get attention in the family depends on it. Additionally, the "victim," or "good" child, imitates their parent and aligns with the parent's judgment of the other child.

In these scenarios, parents believe they are being fair to the children, giving attention and consequences according to each child's behavior. How unfair it may seem to one child who is "good" to not punish a child who is being "bad"! Unfortunately, fairness treats everyone the same, as if they have the same needs. The true needs of each child are missed. Fairness actually does a disservice. If you have the challenge of more than one child in your family, you will find that as you practice the *Chaos to Connection* essentials, your children will follow your example. When you begin to see your "acting out" teen with new eyes, other children will see them with new eyes. Labels will fall away, and you'll make way for new paths to giving your children attention. Your children will each learn self-awareness and have the space to go through emotional cycles and to have their true needs met. Remember that what you are learning will help and can be applied to both the teen with acting out behaviors and other children.

- As a parent, you are a loving leader, creating safety in your home.
- Safety includes relational and emotional safety.
- Emotional safety is providing the space to accept yourself and your child exactly where you or she is in the moment.
- Your practice in awareness and completing emotional cycles creates emotional safety in your family.
- Boundaries are internal and external actions you take to create a safe space to connect. Boundaries differ from rules in that boundaries address your needs and rules are set to control your child.
- The emotional cycle is important for your teen, so he can learn how to return to a place of calm and love through an internal process rather than external soothers.

PERSONAL PRACTICES

1. Choose a physical place that is safe for you, maybe your couch or car, where you can go when you are triggered. Use the safe place as a reminder to create emotional safety. You may have to create emotional safety without your child being emotionally safe. Your child may be yelling or screaming or acting out in other ways while you open the space for him or her to have the emotions. Practice getting into your safe space without shutting your child's experience off.

2. Practice taking care of your own fear. Notice where you feel fear in your body; is there any fear present now? If there is, breathe into it. Connect with the sensation. Does it have a color, a shape, a temperature? What is its consistency? What is the fear trying to communicate to you? Write down whatever thoughts come to mind no matter how random or irrational they seem.

3. Use a phrase to keep focus on yourself when you are triggered by your teen's behavior, such as, "This is not my fault. I am not to blame. Right now [child's name] is scared and hurting. He/she needs my love. How can I take care of myself and be loving with him/her?"

4. Use your triggers to practice awareness. For example, when walking into your teenager's room and witnessing an outrageous mess, you may move into judgment and anger. You might want to bulldoze the mess or slam the door and avoid ever going in there again. Instead, as you walk in, "use" the chaos to check in with your own awareness of judgments, criticisms, and desires for change.

5. Remember an event that triggered you. Describe to yourself or on paper what happened:
- Describe the event, including the facts of what you sensed (seeing, smelling, tasting, touching, and hearing).
- Describe the physical sensations in your body (a "rush," pain, or pressure somewhere).
- Name the emotions you experience based on these interpretations. These may include such emotions as fear, shame, anger, disappointment, judgment.
- Refocus on the physical sensations. Breathe deeply into the areas of discomfort. Take 10 deep breaths, focusing on bringing oxygen to the parts of your body that are experiencing discomfort.
- Notice the interpretations of the events and sensations that your mind made. What were your main thoughts?
- Hold your emotion and imagine embracing it. Let the emotion rise as high as it needs to and hold your emotion. As you hold it, you will feel it recede and feel yourself returning to a place of calm.
- Take a deep breath. Express gratitude for the emotional cycle you went through.
- You may find that you feel shaky or fatigued. Take care of yourself in this place—get a drink of water or treat yourself to a cup of coffee or a smoothie, go for a walk, listen to music, or pick up a good book.

6. Think of a rule that you have set in your family and the expectation behind that rule. Now rethink that expectation—is it about controlling your child or setting a true boundary to have your need met? If your rule is about control, use this time to reset the rule with your new understanding of internal boundaries. You may do away with your rule or you may change it.

7. The following phrases may help you create emotional safety:
- Say to yourself, "Wow. That was a strong response to what she did. I wonder what's going on. Why was that response so strong? What is the feeling? What does that feeling tell me about what I need?"

- To express curiosity with your teen, say, "I'd love to hear about your experience if you want to share."
- To give yourself space to work with an emotion, use self-talk: "Whose anger (or other emotion) is it? It's mine. My anger is mine, my child's anger is his. And who needs to work with it? I do. Because I'm not getting my needs met. I need to work with my anger so I don't give it to him."

"Oh, the comfort—the inexpressible comfort of feeling safe with a person—having neither to weigh thoughts nor measure words, but pouring them all right out, just as they are, chaff and grain together; certain that a faithful hand will take and sift them, keep what is worth keeping, and then with the breath of kindness blow the rest away."

DINAH CRAIK

3

SUPPORT

sup·port *(verb)*: to promote the interests or cause of, to uphold or defend as valid or right; to hold up or serve as a foundation or prop for; to keep from fainting, yielding, or losing courage; to receive help.

We are wired to be in relationships. Our whole heart, body, and mind crave connection with others to share our life. We desire people with whom we can express our joys, our problems, our successes, our sadness, our celebrations. As you are making changes in how you relate to your child and react to their behaviors, having friends and support are key elements to your success. Your connections will eventually help you connect to your child. You can get the support you need by recognizing this need, reaching out, and being vulnerable.

RECOGNIZING THE NEED For families who are struggling with their teen's behavior, the focus on support is usually on the teen. Just as parents sacrifice their self-awareness and self-care, parents often ignore their need for support and sacrifice time and energy that could go toward gaining support to focus on their teen. The reality is that you and your teen both need support. Both of you need a safe place—a safe sounding board or connection—where you can feel validated and be heard without judgment. It is important to remember that both your needs and your teen's needs are equally important.

The first step to getting support is recognizing your limitations and your need for support. Often when we are under intense stress we have a hard time recognizing this need and what would be supportive. You may even wait so long to get support that you feel like you are drowning. Your need for support is not about finding someone who can fix your problems or your emotional state, but finding someone who can be your sounding board and a reflector to help you process.

Intuitively, each one of us craves the kind of connection in which we can be seen, heard, and validated. We want a friend or several friends who really know us. Such a need becomes even greater in times of stress. Indeed, research has found that women and men have different stress responses. Due to different hormones, men tend to have a "fight-or-flight" response, and women have a "tend-and-befriend" response in which they respond to stress by nurturing and going to friends or social groups. The "tend-and-befriend" response actually reduces the hormonal response so women can stay calm under stress! Women naturally create, maintain, and use their support to manage stressful conditions. Your need for support is natural.[1]

Additionally, as described in Chapter 1: Awareness, parents often try to fix their child's behavior in order to feel better. It is not unusual for parents to discover that some of their conflict with their teen arises from their own need to be seen, heard, and validated. But parents can fulfill some of this need through close relationships with other adults who provide validation and love.

As an example of support and how it can help you, read the following story about a mother so focused on her daughter completing her chores that she was unaware of what was truly going on:

> Kim, a single mother, was having a hard time engaging her daughter, Sally, to help her with chores around the house. Kim had laid out what she expected Sally to help with, had made a list she kept on the refrigerator, and reminded Sally frequently of her chores. But Sally refused to help. Since making the list, whenever Kim asked Sally to do her chores, Sally got angry—yelling, calling her mother names, retreating to her room and pretending to do homework, and once threatening to hit Kim. The more overwhelmed Kim felt, the more needy she became and began to demand that Sally do her chores or she would ground her. The more Sally felt the pressure to meet her mother's needs, the more she acted out and wouldn't do what Kim asked. The relationship between them quickly deteriorated.

In the above story, we see a parent who has made reasonable requests of her daughter to help around the house. Let's take another look at this story after Kim has practiced awareness, created a Grace Gap, and sought support:

> Seeing that the pattern in their relationship was getting them nowhere and actually ruining their relationship, Kim made a commitment to become aware of her needs that arose when she became over-focused on the housework, namely needing to be heard and validated. She decided to call her friend Sue every time she wanted to force Sally into doing her chores. Her focus of the call was to share with Sue how overwhelmed she felt instead of complaining about what a "bad" kid Sally was. Each time Kim did this, she began to notice that when Sally came home she was able to relax around her

intense need. As she did, amazingly enough, Sally began to offer more support around the house.

In getting the support she needed to deal with her overwhelming feelings, Kim was able to engage herself and Sally in a relationship that began to support them both.

REACHING OUT Now that you know the importance of support, you can learn to recognize when to reach out for support. Using your awareness in the present moment, you can discover how you are feeling and assess your stress tolerance. You may be beginning to move through your emotions, learning to sit with them until they subside. Now you can also help yourself in trigger moments by reaching out for support from a friend or partner to jump-start your journey inward. It will be especially important to reach out to a support person when you find yourself reaching out to your teen to fulfill your needs.

The support you need can take many forms, and different support people will play different roles. Part of your job in taking care of yourself is to gather around you all the people you need to take care of your heart, body, and mind. These may include close friends, a spouse or partner, family members, in-person or online support groups, doctors, religious or spiritual leaders, professional counselors, massage therapists, fitness instructors, house cleaners, etc. The ability to support yourself and to take responsibility for your own happiness during challenging times is empowering.

A true friend, whether related or not, sees your authentic self in the midst of your distress and does not lose sight of your innate strengths and qualities. If and when you lose sight of your gifts, a true friend can help you remember them and how to move forward. A close friend can also help you feel safe, valued, and loved just because you are you. One of the best supports is a friend you can call when you are in the midst of really strong emotions. Such friends can support you and help you create a Grace Gap. It is important to find a friend or other support person who is empathic to your feelings and who provides an unconditionally loving presence, but who does not feed any feelings of powerlessness or of being a victim.

A good support person often "just" listens, holding you until you've worn yourself out and reminding you who you truly are. The following story provides an example of good support:

Ann called Rosa one morning and told her that she was feeling like a victim of her son, husband, and life. That morning, her husband had complained that Ann hadn't gone shopping recently and there was no food for him to eat for breakfast. Her son sprang on her that he needed new football cleats for practice that day. On top of that, Ann had a big deadline at work, one of their toilets was clogged, and the dog was vomiting. Ann described the events and her feelings of anger, frustration, and powerlessness. Rosa listened, without judgment, to all that Ann was describing, validating Ann's feelings and experience while not agreeing that she was powerless. Ann could feel Rosa opening up to her, hearing, seeing, and validating her experience. Ann continued to talk, cry, and rage on the phone until she had nothing else to say. Along the way, Rosa asked her questions, "How were you feeling when that happened? Oh Ann, so much anger and stress! I can feel it! What else, is there more? How are you doing now?" Rosa was there to support her seeing the truth behind all of her feelings. "Ann, my friend, I love you. You are such a wonderful mother, and I know you are angry. I can feel it! Thank you for sharing with me."

As you seek support, you may feel pressure to share and be open with your family. But family dynamics can be complicated, and if a family member is not helpful and increases your fear, shame, or judgment, remember that you are not obligated to share with him or her. Whomever you choose to reach out to, the most important part of reaching out is choosing a safe place where you can be seen, heard, and validated, and yet not encouraged to blame your feelings on external things or other people.

In-person and online support groups may also be helpful to you. Support groups provide a safe place to give and receive emotional and practical support. Knowing that other parents have similar situations, that you're not the only one, that your response is common (and you're not "crazy"), and that you have a place to vent can be validating and relieving. You can find a variety of support groups, including those led by untrained parents or trained professionals, and those that are educational and structured or less formal and designed for personal sharing. Online support groups include blogs, message boards, electronic newsletters, and chat rooms. In finding the right support group for you, look for groups that match your needs and personality. If a group doesn't match your needs or feel right, seek out another group.

Professional support in the form of doctors, religious leaders, and trained practitioners can provide assistance, if you or your child need medical assistance, or if you or your child need additional assistance processing and working through your experience (see Common Challenges below for information on choosing a trained practitioner for your child).

Finally, you might have as part of your support team people that you pay to help. Massage sessions and exercise are great ways to take a break from all the heart work and emotional intensity in your life so you can refill. When life is chaotic, it can be so helpful to have someone who can help you with things like house and yard work.

With these suggestions of the kinds of support available, get curious about what kind of support you need. In a dream world, who would be part of that team? If there were no fear, shame, or judgment, who would you call? If money were not an issue, who would you hire to help? Be creative in how you can incorporate these into your daily life. And then consider who will be true support to have on your team.

LEARNING TO BE SUPPORTIVE

Reaching out and receiving support requires that you become vulnerable in front of another person. As we have said, you were made to be in relationships, and being in relationships means sharing your heart with others. A variety of factors may prevent you from being naturally vulnerable, including messages you received as you were growing up and messages you receive as a parent. Growing up, you may have heard that you need to be self-reliant or were praised for being strong and independent. You may also have been taught that it is not safe to be vulnerable and reach out, possibly experiencing shame, punishment, or having love withdrawn for your vulnerability. If you were too vulnerable, you may have been called weak or told you cry too much. In all of these messages, your vulnerability was not valued but seen as negative.

With the pressure to be a good parent and even a "super" parent, parents can fall into a trap of thinking they need to handle everything themselves or handle everything within the family. Within families who are struggling with a teen's behavior, reaching out for support can be even more difficult because it means dealing with fear, judgment, and shame about a child's behavior and allowing another person to see these struggles.

The truth is that your vulnerability can guide you to a greater truth about yourself and relationships with other people. Your vulnerability is a tool that can inform you when you need support and a tool to getting the support you need. Your vulnerability also moves you into better relationships with people, from a place of shame and hiding to a place of openness, where you can be held and seen and come to know yourself better.

You may need to reset how you think of your vulnerability. Think about a time when a close friend or your partner was vulnerable with you. What did you learn? How did you feel? How did you feel afterward? Perhaps you learned more about your friend, her likes and dislikes, about her childhood, about her view of the world. Perhaps you felt a little uncomfortable while your friend was being so vulnerable, but most likely you didn't think he should not tell you and deal with his own stuff by himself. Perhaps afterward you felt closer to your friend, having learned something new and deeper about him. True friends value your vulnerability.

We assure you that you have or can develop the skills to get the support you need, and that getting support for yourself will open you to new possibilities of relating. Reaching out to others, especially if you are not used to being vulnerable or have withdrawn from others as things declined with your teen, can be scary. Remember that you have already started the work in knowing your own heart and in handling fear, shame, and judgment. In seeking support, you increase your self-love because you are taking care of yourself. There is no shame in getting the support and help you need. We know that there are people who want to know your heart, who want to hear about your experience, including your struggles as well as your joys.

One of the benefits of getting support for yourself is gaining a deep sense of how giving support is done. While you're getting support, try putting your newly expanded awareness to work. Pay attention to what good and supportive interactions feel like. You might notice, for example, that sincere, caring people habitually adopt an open posture. Their body language tells you they are open to what you have to say. They don't respond to your statements with judgments or well-meaning practical solutions. They ask open-ended questions and may prompt you for more information, to go a little deeper. They don't feel compelled to respond to everything you say. Sometimes they respond with a rephrasing of something you just said, giving you just enough new information to lead you to a new idea.

At this point with your teen, if you are unable to offer support, continue to practice awareness with your teen, knowing your emotions, creating a Grace Gap, and providing an open place for your teen to be. Your work on connecting with others will continue to move you to a place where you can better connect with your child.

We find that parents share common challenges to finding and receiving support including: the belief that the focus should be on their teen, difficulty reaching out, the fear of vulnerability, the stress put on partners, and the need for support for the teen.

You may find, as you are thinking about the support you need and gathering people around you, that you run into the belief that "It's not about me. It's my teen's problem." Such a belief will be a challenge and limit your discovery of other possibilities. It is also an opportunity to return to key teachings from Chapter 1: Awareness. The best way to take care of your child is to take care of yourself. You are helping your teen by seeking support, just as you help your teen by growing your awareness and improving your self-care.

If you have trouble reaching out for support, it may be helpful to start by reframing what it means to get support. Typically, the hesitation to reach out stems from feelings of shame, not being good enough, or being afraid of being too much for another person to handle. We as humans are designed to live in groups, as we have since prehistoric times.[2] Research has also shown that living in connected groups helps young people thrive; and other adult relationships and caring neighbors are important developmental assets for children.[3] In community, no one set of parents is the sole provider of parenting to their children. It is unreasonable to expect to parent effectively without community because the extended support system helps everyone to get their needs met more effectively. Families need help from other families![4] Reaching out for support is nothing to be ashamed of or to fear. Reaching out for support is part of your human nature. A true friend wants you to be vulnerable, wants to know these parts of you, and knows how to handle you.

Parenting teens can be a stressful experience, especially when making changes to your way of parenting. Too often, stress around parenting creates conflict between partners rather than bringing them closer together, and can be a challenge as you reach out for support. It is important to practice good self-care, and if you are married or in a relationship, to take good care of your partnership. This challenge is an opportunity to promote greater intimacy and love in your couple relationship. Experiment with these guidelines:

- Be able to discern in the moment if your partner is the best person to share your emotional experience with. Sometimes it is more effective to share your intense feelings with a friend who may be more neutral and less personally affected. You can then discuss your experience with your partner when you are calmer.
- Make sure you have sources of support that are outside of the relationship. No partner is ever able to be present all of the time or to meet all of your needs.
- When you ask your partner for emotional support, be genuinely able to accept their "yes" or "no" response.
- If your partner's response is "no," do your best to recognize that this is not a personal rejection, but your partner taking care of herself. Remind yourself that her self-care supports the two of you having a healthy, intimate relationship that is sustainable.
- Remember that when external support is not available, you can always reach inward for your own

support. Develop your ability to use internal self-talk and the other self-soothing techniques you've learned that are supportive and loving toward yourself.

By remembering these guidelines and suggestions for how to use your partner for support, you both can continue to take care of yourselves and to offer each other support.

We recognize that as you are finding support for yourself, you may also want to find support for your teen. Often, a trained practitioner can provide the most effective support for your teen, especially if your teen's behavior is consistently dangerous or violent. If you need to pursue professional help for your teen, we recommend finding an organization or practitioner who provides:

- Family system-oriented treatment.
- Helping your teen work with his emotions.
- Relational and strengths-based treatment rather than behavior modification treatment. Such treatment may sound like a good option, but we have found that without working on the underlying cause of the behavior, the behavior may return when the teen is under stress.
- Heart-centered parenting styles.

Trust yourself in choosing whether or not you seek treatment for your teen and what kind of treatment you choose. If you choose to pursue treatment for your teen, your participation will continue to be fundamental. You will need to be an active participant in treatment and the treatment plan, be open to looking at how you contribute to the current family dynamics, and be willing to do your own work while your teen is in treatment. Re-building and creating a safe emotional relationship with yourself will be the greatest support you can provide.

KEY LEARNINGS
- Both your needs and your teen's needs are equally important.
- You need, crave, and deserve supportive relationships.
- You can get the support you need by recognizing your need, reaching out, and being vulnerable.
- Gather around you friends and professionals who can provide the support you need.
- Support will help you in your efforts toward self-care as well as develop your ability to support others.

• Consider a trained practitioner for help if you or your teen is destructive or violent.

1. Identify those around you who can provide positive support and who can be there for you when you are at your worst (raging, tearful, yelling, swearing).

2. The following dialogue may help you to start the conversation to ask for support:

"Hi, I am having a challenging day, do you have time to listen?"

"Hi, I'm feeling so angry right now I need to vent, can you talk?"

"Hi, I really want to escape right now, do you have time to hear me out?"

"Hi, my kids are driving me crazy! I need to vent, do you have a minute?"

3. Have a point person set up to call when you are triggered by your teen's behavior. Even if your friend isn't home, just making a commitment to get the true support you need will begin to shift your focus toward getting support from someone that can be there instead of expecting your teen to be there for you.

4. Use the following prompts to become aware of what you say to yourself, daily or when your teen's behavior triggers you, and what your beliefs are around them.

• Do stream of consciousness writing for 20 minutes. Write whatever comes to your mind without worrying whether it makes sense.

• Listen for limiting beliefs that come up (i.e. I am a bad person. I am hopeless. I am a failure. I am a bad parent. I am not good enough. I am worthless. I am powerless), especially for those that come up repeatedly.

• Identify what is true (i.e. I am good. I have hope. I am a success. I am a good parent. I am good enough. I am worthy. I am powerful. I didn't behave how I would have liked to in that situation).

• Use the true statements as self-talk to support yourself. You have the power to support your emotional needs.

5. Practice releasing emotional energy. Use the following prompts to guide yourself through physically releasing emotional energy:

• Become aware of your body. Feel where you are holding yourself in a tight, constricted way. Notice where in your body or if all of your body is hard with your energy pulled in. You may feel that you have large barriers up to protect you from the external thing causing you discomfort (a person, a situation, etc.).

- Exaggerate the hold by squeezing everything in your body as tight as you can. Hold for 30 seconds and release. Feel the difference between the squeeze and openness. Feel the power you have to choose to squeeze and to be open.
- Begin to make circles in your lower body, allowing the energy to move. Avoid labeling the energy.
- Become curious. With self-talk, tell your body it's okay to move out of the constricted state.
- Feel where the energy moves to and watch it. See how that part of the body responds to the energy and let your body express the feeling it's holding. This may look like making sounds, pushing your hands onto the floor, kicking, shaking your head. Let the energy move out of your body as you move.
- As the energy releases your feeling, you may find the words behind it. Listen to the words and the need behind it, perhaps being valued, being taken care of, being respected, being heard, being validated.
- Sit with the words and the need that surfaces. Realize that this is a valid need, and you can take care of it. You can value yourself, take care of yourself, respect yourself, hear yourself. Imagine taking the power back from the external thing that caused discomfort. You may feel more open and at peace.
- Know that such a feeling will not go away quickly. It may be set off again by something external, but you will begin to move faster through the feeling and back to a state of calm.

"Thus nature has no love for solitude, and always leans, as it were, on some support; and the sweetest support is found in the most intimate friendship."

CICERO

II

re·viv·ing *(verb)*: restoring to consciousness or life; restoring from a depressed, inactive, or unused state; using awareness, safety, and support to restore your child's heart.

Your practice in awareness, safety, and support has led your family out of the emergency room. At home, as you redress wounds and continue to treat yourself, you are ready to learn more essentials and to begin interacting more with your child. Take a moment to feel gratitude for yourself for all that you have done for yourself, your child, and your family.

The next three heart-centered essentials are found in Reviving, a mode in which your family functioning has improved due to the practice you have done in awareness, safety, and support. You may be wondering how to know if your practice is really working and if you are moving from Surviving and into Reviving. The following comparison of the two modes will show you the progress you are making.

SURVIVING	REVIVING
High stress.	Improved ability to handle high stress even as the intensity in your family may build.
Intense emotions and emotional reactions.	Stopping, sitting, and breathing. Creating a gap.
	Realizing, "I am not the feelings. I am separate from the experience itself."
Recurring physical reactions.	Taking care of yourself and doing wellness checks.
Feeling out of control, powerless, and desperate.	Feeling less out-of-control, regaining personal power.
Feeling like a victim.	Feeling more confident, grounded, and ready to meet new challenges.
	Feeling like you're moving forward.
Intolerance, rigidness, lack of empathy, and a black and white view of situations.	Dropping judgment and increasing curiosity about yourself and your teen.
Disconnection from physical sensations and yourself.	Connecting to physical sensations to notice triggers and stress.
	Sometimes looking at yourself from the outside and naming what's going on.
	Starting to notice yourself and being aware of your emotional reactivity.
	Working with your emotions in a more positive way with awareness, support and safety.
Feeling like a hostage in your own home.	Starting to enjoy being in your home.
Focus on teen behavior.	Focusing on yourself even as your teen does not change his acting out behavior.
Operating from your head and not your heart.	Using your heart lens and increasing emotional safety.
Thinking that this is never going to change, and it is always going to be difficult.	Feeling like you're in foreign territory in transition as you practice unconditional love.
Desperate to begin learning Chaos to Connection.	Questioning yourself and doubting the Chaos to Connection process.

When you are Reviving, you interpret your child's behavior differently than when you were Surviving. Rather than seeing your child's behavior as disrespectful, defiant, lazy, or dishonest, you begin to see with your heart lens that your child is in distress, is saying no, has low self-confidence, or is in fear of getting in trouble. Unlike in Surviving when your child's behavior sent you into an intense emotional state, you now know how to Stop, Sit, and Breathe and to let your feelings surface.

In this second section, we will define, discuss, illustrate, and provide practice for three parenting essentials that will begin this Reviving process. These three fundamentals are **Presence, Engagement,** and **Guidance.**

Whereas you, the parent, are the focus when you are Surviving, your child becomes the focus when you are Reviving, but in a new, heart-centered way and without forgetting yourself. You will continue as the loving leader you are learning to be. When you are Reviving, it is much like doing the dishes by hand. You soak the pots, pans, and dishes, and all the junk eventually comes loose and surfaces. In the process, the dishes and water look dirtier and messier, but you are cleaning more deeply and know that eventually the dishes will be free of grime.

As you move through the three modes of *Chaos to Connection*, remember that you will reenter all three modes to some degree—immersed or just dipping your toe—and you will continue to use what you develop in each mode.

"When it is dark enough,
you can see the stars."

RALPH WALDO EMERSON

4

PRESENCE

pres·ence *(noun)*: the fact or condition of being present; the part of space within one's immediate vicinity; the bearing, carriage, or air of a person; providing a personal state of peace in which everything can be accepted.

You may have a number of emotions as you think about turning your attention from yourself to your child. You may feel relief, anxiety, happiness, or all of the above. Before we dive into describing and learning about presence, take time to check in with yourself using the Wellness Check or Personal Practices in Chapter 1: Awareness.

As you do the work of building awareness and taking care of yourself, your child may regress or her behavior may escalate. You may get feedback that your child's behavior is getting worse, and they may question your new way of parenting. But the changes you see in your child are her reactions to the positive changes you are making with awareness, safety, and support. Though your child's behavior presents challenges (or opportunities in disguise), they are a good sign that you are showing up and connecting. When you take care of yourself, you become emotionally safe, and you shift the pattern of love in your family. Your child may feel abandoned because the old patterns have changed, and he may try his hardest to engage in the old pattern of love, acting out to see if you will fall back also. This is your opportunity to practice what you have learned and to further shift and grow. Recommitment to the process you have started with *Chaos to Connection* may help you, and we have provided suggestions for recommitment in the Personal Practices at the end of this chapter.

You can continue the work you've started to help your teen by developing your presence. Your presence is vitally important to improving your relationship with your teen. Much of your communication with your teen is based not on the words you speak but on your emotional state, because teens operate on an emotional level. They feel the world. Your presence—your internal state of being—speaks to your teen. If your presence is angry, your teen will hear anger. If your presence is fearful, your teen will hear fear. He will hear your emotions regardless of what your words say. If your presence is emotionally safe, loving, and peaceful, it is a powerful healing force.

In learning presence, you will interact with your teen in a new way, at a heart-level. We will begin with a story to give you a picture of what presence looks like:

Becky had been out of the house for weeks and living on the streets. She didn't want to come home because when she did, she got a lecture from her parents, Steve and Diane. Steve and Diane were constantly worried about their daughter and wanted to change her behavior. But all the lecturing only made things worse. They began to understand that they needed to work on their awareness and becoming emotionally safe before approaching Becky. When they were ready to spend time with Becky, they decided to change how they interacted with her. They started by meeting her for coffee. They spent the time just chatting and enjoying her company. Becky would leave and go back out on the streets, but over time they began to notice a difference in the relationship.

One night, Steve and Diane heard noises upstairs in Becky's room and knew Becky was sneaking into her room. They resisted the impulse to go up to the room and interact with Becky. Instead, they both focused on creating a loving presence within the home, and expanding it all the way upstairs. They didn't move physically, they just stayed still, being as present and loving as they could. Over the span of a week, Becky started to come downstairs for breakfast. Again, they didn't talk about the past, or lecture her on what she was doing or not doing. They stayed focused on their loving presence. Within a month, Becky was back home, engaging in every family meal, going to school, and opening up in new ways to her mom.

Steve and Diane's work on awareness and developing a loving presence made the change in the relationship between Becky and themselves possible.

Are you wondering what exactly presence means? Presence in heart-centered parenting is your "air," or the feeling you give to others. In our interactions with other people, there is a primary level of verbal communication. There are also nonverbal cues we give about who we are, how we are feeling, or what state we are in (frustration, peace, agitation, happiness) through body language, tone of voice, eye contact, and touch. These nonverbal cues reveal our presence. You have likely met people who on the first impression gave you either an uneasy or a warm feeling. You sensed their presence.

With someone you know well, such as a spouse, partner or a close friend, you know without talking if he is in a good or bad mood. You feel his or her presence.

Presence has another aspect: being present in the moment. A loving presence needs to be loving and available. You make your loving presence available no matter what emotional state she is in (i.e., angry, happy, sad, or excited). You make your loving presence available by setting aside distractions (cell phones, television, books, work, other people), the past (what your teen did three months ago), and the future (what your teen might do based on present behavior). You step aside from everything else except sinking into the moment with your teen. In having a loving presence, you portray, "I can love my child right now. I can handle you, whatever you bring."

To provide a loving presence to your child, like Becky's parents in the story above, you will need to unconditionally love, to heal old wounds, to release limiting beliefs, and to practice acceptance. We will begin with unconditional love.

UNCONDITIONAL LOVE

As you learned about emotional safety for yourself and your teen, you also learned about unconditional love. When you unconditionally love another person, you love her regardless of her actions or beliefs, exactly where she is. When you conditionally love another person, you love her when she acts or believes as you want her to believe. In effect, if the behavior or beliefs are not what you want, you withdraw love and open the door to fear. You *can* unconditionally love your teen. To grow your unconditional love:

- Use your awareness to recognize that your triggers, awakened in response to your teen's behavior, are more about you than about them.
- Use your awareness to work on yourself—to move through your emotions and return to calm and love—before attending to your child.
- Learn to unconditionally love your own negative reactions and judgments to a behavior, so that you can offer an unconditionally loving response to your child.
- Remember, your teen is behaving exactly in the appropriate way for the emotional state he is experiencing. As adults when we are in distress, we don't stop to think of what appropriate behavior we need to exhibit so

others will feel okay. And yet, we ask our kids to do this very thing.

- Interact with your child with curiosity—a sense of, so what was that like? How was that for you? What did you get out of that? She is less likely to put up boundaries and barriers. You give her space where she doesn't have to hide her actions or emotions to be safe.

Part of developing unconditional love involves bringing awareness to your feelings and improving your emotional state when you are triggered. Triggers actually arise from old wounds and limiting beliefs, which need to be healed or released so you can be present.

When triggers arise from old wounds, you may find yourself reacting and feeling as you did as a child. When your child exhibits a behavior that you were shamed or judged for, for example, you regress to your own past, to the experience in which you were wounded. You usually deal with your child in that instance the way you were dealt with, as a child, reacting from an old wound.

Along with old wounds, you also have limiting beliefs. Limiting beliefs are those opinions, philosophical principles, and messages you picked up as a child or adult that seem true but no longer serve you. These may include beliefs about yourself such as "I'm not good enough," "My emotions are too big for other people to handle," or "I'm a bad parent." These may include beliefs about things, "Video games are bad" or about your child, "If my child doesn't graduate college, he won't make anything of his life." Limiting beliefs prevent you from connecting with your child. If you continue to interact with your child under the limiting belief that video games are bad, for example, your actions will be directed at getting rid of the video games rather than connecting to your child. Likewise, if you interact with your child under the belief that you're not good enough, you will seek validation and worth from your child rather than connecting.

We all have old wounds and limiting beliefs from our past. You can look at your beliefs and see if they are serving you. You might discover a belief and ask, "Is it true? Do I want to continue living under this belief?" You can also go back and repair your childhood experiences, nurturing yourself in the way you may have missed as a child to change your belief. Through such nurturing you can then provide a loving presence for your teen. Such healing does not have to be in a lengthy verbal exploration; just the willingness to acknowledge your vulnerability as an adult is enough. Consider the story of one dad who worked to heal old wounds:

> Dan's son, Ian, had rejected his father's religious community and friends, refusing to go with his father to worship, to get together with his friends, or to participate in the community's groups for boys his age. Dan was enraged! He started withdrawing his love for Ian and finding ways to avoid being with him. Then with support, Dan started to be curious about his reaction to Ian and why it was so strong. On the one hand, he could understand Ian wanting to make his own choices about his faith and community, but on the other hand, he was so angry about Ian's decision. As he thought about it, he began to get in touch with the lonely boy inside him that was often ignored by his parents. He described to his wife his desire as a boy to be a part of community rather than walking alone to and from school and synagogue. As an adult, he created a great support system through his temple and friends. When Ian rejected this community, he felt like the lonely boy again, like the boy who felt ignored by his parents.

> Dan took his healing one step further. He described his fantasy around being a happy boy, a classic image of playing ball with his dad. Dan actually played out his fantasy by going to a baseball field with a friend, wearing a baseball cap and glove and playing some baseball. All the while, Dan told the lonely boy inside him that the adult Dan was taking care of him.

Like Dan, you likely have old wounds that need healing. When you heal your old wounds and release limiting beliefs, you are able to be open and loving with your teen.

ACCEPTANCE

To have a loving presence with your teen, you also need to practice acceptance. By acceptance, we mean acceptance of "what is" rather than wanting your teen to be different. Because so many of your behaviors were judged, you find yourself sitting in judgment of your teen's negative behavior. Instead of accepting what is, in the moment, you desperately want to shift it because of the discomfort it brings up for you. You fall back into old beliefs that convince you that if only you can shift your teen's behavior you will feel like a good parent. To stand in total acceptance of the behavior and the moment allows you to stay open and truly hear the communication that lies beneath the behavior. Only then do you have a chance to meet the underlying need that is driving the negative behavior. Accepting "what is" and being present in the moment is the doorway to shifting your child's state of being from one of fear to love.

As you are processing unconditional love, healing old wounds, and acceptance, consider the following story of a father who practiced these and offered his daughter a loving presence:

> Jim was having breakfast with his daughter Emma one morning. She wasn't very talkative so he gave her space. When Emma moved her arm to get a box of cereal, he noticed some cuts on her arm that looked like self-inflicted cuts. This was the first time he had seen the cuts, and he felt a charge of fear about what this meant and a rush of thoughts about what would happen to his daughter if she kept doing this. He felt shame that he had "let" his daughter get to this point. But instead of yelling and running to get help, he maintained a state of love and just caressed her arm. In a low voice, he said, "Darling, where was I?" Emma was surprised by his response. He maintained the openness, and he said, "I'm so sorry that I wasn't there with you, but I'm here now. I'm here to help you hold some of that pain. Where does it hurt?"

Seeing the cuts on Emma's arm was alarming to Jim and set off alarms about him as a parent and his daughter's future; but rather than react out of his triggers, Jim chose to work with his triggers, to offer unconditional love and to accept what is, the cuts on his daughter's arm and her emotional pain. Doing so, he could come to his daughter with a presence of love, a state of being in which his daughter had the opportunity to feel and share her emotions. She did not need to fear her father's reaction.

In a loving presence, you give your child the opportunity to move through the emotional cycle, to have all the strong, intense feeling she needs to return to love. Your child then can feel all she needs to feel to return to a place of calm and love because of your presence. You have brought what you've learned in awareness and safety to your child.

As you develop a loving presence for your child, you may find that you experience some of the common challenges parents experience, including reacting from your trigger, lacking authenticity in your presence, wanting to interrupt your child's emotional cycle, and overdoing presence.

One of the challenges that you may experience is reacting from a trigger (notice this characteristic of Surviving) rather than creating a Grace Gap to calm yourself and being with your child in an unconditionally loving way. Don't be discouraged. None of us can have a peaceful, loving presence at all times, especially when you are stressed, tired, or hungry, and you will make mistakes. It is important to continue taking care of yourself—your heart and your body. If you are triggered, tell your teen, "I'm triggered right now. I'm [name your feeling]. I can't go any further right now."

You may be anxious to be present for your child, but take care that you avoid covering up your emotions. If your presence and words do not align, this can cause confusion and stress for your child as she senses one thing (i.e., you're still in a place of fear or anger) and hears another (i.e., "I'm not afraid. I am here for you without judgment."). Your presence needs to be authentically loving to be healing. As you work on your self-awareness, you are also working on being more authentic, knowing and moving through your true feelings to return to love and to a place where you interact out of love rather than triggers. Instead of hiding your feelings, reveal them to your teen and share how you feel. You might say, "I get so scared that something is going to happen to you when you stay out late" or "When you were smoking pot, I was afraid you were going to become a drug addict." Remember to own your feelings, "These are my feelings. You didn't cause them and you can't fix them." Rather than being blaming or controlling, sharing your feelings gives your teen a chance to understand you.

In the work you have done, you may have a time when your child, for the first time in a long time, has the opportunity to go through the full emotional cycle from intense feeling back to calm. Being with your child as he goes through the emotional cycle can be a frightening experience. His emotions will be extreme and intense. As a loving parent, you may feel the urge to rush in and help relieve his emotions, to do or give something to stop his cycle. This is a natural feeling. But the best thing you can do is focus all the energy you would put toward doing and giving on your presence instead. Concentrate on making your presence unconditionally loving and accepting. Imagine your love as "holding" your child. Your child will calm himself, and being able to go through the cycle in your loving presence will be healing for both of you.

As your teen starts to move toward you, you may wonder how present you should be in your teen's life and even have an inclination to increase your presence significantly. While you want to be present and available to your teen, it is important to not be overbearing. Begin by taking your teen's lead in how present you should be and how much to increase your presence. Your teen may or may not like periodic check-ins by text or phone. Your teen may or may not like having regular dates or times when you spend time together. Take your teen's lead so that your presence remains about your teen and not about your need to be in contact.

KEY LEARNINGS

- Presence is your "air," bearing, or the feeling you give to others.
- Presence is being authentically loving.
- Presence is being present in the moment.
- A loving and peaceful presence is a powerful healing force.
- You can provide a loving presence to your teen by offering unconditional love, healing your old wounds, and accepting "what is."

PERSONAL PRACTICES

1. Write a letter to yourself as a recommitment practice. Write about why you are practicing the *Chaos to Connection* essentials. Remember the events that led you to picking up this book. Now write about what is bringing you joy and what you like and don't like about practicing the essentials.

2. Enter a room where your family is and try not to be noticed. Make your presence as little as you can and see what you notice as you enter the room. Check in with how you feel, what thoughts are going on in your mind. Just see what it is like to be able to have control over your presence.

Next enter into a room where your family is and come in with a big voice, large energy, and a huge presence. Check in with how you feel, what are you thoughts, and where does your attention move?

3. Write down your fears about your teen, such as "I'm afraid Emily is doing drugs" or "I'm afraid Emily is skipping school." Then go back to each item on the list and replace "afraid" with "curious." Your statements become, "I am curious about whether Emily is doing drugs," "I am curious about whether Emily is skipping school," and so on. See whether you feel any differently about these things and whether you shift from fear to acceptance. Does being curious make it easier to think about them? Can you imagine talking to your teen about these things?

4. When your family is Reviving, and your teen's behavior seems to be regressing or getting worse, you may have people around you who question your decision to be a heart-centered parent. The following points may help you to describe heart-centered parenting to others:

- Heart-centered parenting is really different from conventional models of parenting, and you feel it is aligned more with how you've always wanted to be with your child.
- The focus is on taking responsibility for how you feel rather than reacting to your child's behavior.
- In the past you focused on the behavior and "how" your teen looked, because we were taught this was part of being a responsible parent.
- You see behavior as communication in heart-centered parenting and try to see what is driving the behavior.
- In heart-centered parenting, you stay more connected to what is going on inside of you.
- Focusing only on getting rid of the behavior does not help your child in the end, because the behavior will show up somewhere else if the root cause is not discovered and addressed.
- You want to "be" with your child, supporting her in finding her own heart path, more than teaching her a lesson.
- It's like seeing your child through fresh eyes, seeing from the heart into your child's heart. When you see from the heart, you are relaxed and open to being there for your child. When you see from your mind, you see from the past or project into the future.

5. Use the following prompts for healing an old wound:

- Remember or notice the next time your teen's behavior triggers you. Be present to yourself and bring awareness to uncover the feeling behind it (anger, fear, sadness).
- Is the feeling old or new? If it is old, continue being curious about the feeling and remember yourself as a child. What did you look like? What did you say? How does your present feeling relate to you as a child? What did you need that you didn't receive?
- As an adult, be curious about how you can take care of the child inside you and take action to care for your child (reassuring self-talk, fulfilling a dream or want, self-care).
- Shift how you think of this wound from an injury to a gift, knowing that you can be present to it and have the strength to face the wound and move forward.

6. Use the following prompts for a guided meditation:

- Find a quiet time in your day. Remove all other possible distractions.
- Think back to the moment when you first felt a deep and unconditionally loving connection with your child. It may have been just after birth, sometime later, or even sometime before.
- What were you doing? Remember the details. What did it feel like? What did it smell like? What did you hear?
- Surrender to that moment. Experience the connection fully. Give it the time it deserves. Breathe slowly and deeply.
- When you are ready, remember that there was something else that made that moment special—the absence of expectations for yourself and your child. Stay with this feeling. Remember what it feels like.

"Absence sharpens love,
presence strengthens it."

BENJAMIN FRANKLIN

5

ENGAGEMENT

en·gage·ment *(noun)*: the act of engaging; emotional involvement or commitment; the state of being in gear; being in another's space; being together with mutual needs and connection.

Presence provides the background work of how to better interact with your child, laying a foundation of unconditional love and acceptance in which to be with your child. As you change how you interact with yourself and your teen, you will likely have more engagement with your child. This is exciting! You may have been waiting for this moment, to engage with your teen or to have your teen engage with you. But this may also be scary! You may want to know how to best engage with your child and to continue the journey you have started.

Before we discuss how to enhance engagement with your child, let's take a look at what engagement is. When two people engage, they choose to join together—to connect—and to do so with equal needs and without a power struggle. As you know already, you and your child both have needs, and neither of your needs is more important than the other's. As you engage, you bring your needs and the ability to fulfill some and to postpone or give up others. Neither you nor your child will have power over the other. You meet your child where he is and in his space without needing to hold power over him, to change his behavior, to meet your needs, or to make you feel better. You realize your child's behavior is communicating a need that has not been met, and you meet those needs.

To illustrate engagement, let's look at a story in which a mom does not engage with her daughter but focuses on controlling her behavior:

> Ellen, who had struggled with drugs and alcohol, fought every rule her mom Nancy set about school, boys, and curfews, and had ultimately been sent to a treatment program. Ellen did really well while she was at the treatment center, revealing again the happy and creative girl that she was. Nancy was so excited about her daughter coming home and having the opportunity to be with her daughter again. She thought that when Ellen returned home she would continue to behave better and would abide by the rules, bringing home what she'd learned in treatment. But within weeks of being back home with the rules in place, Ellen was back to using drugs and alcohol and staying out past curfew or not coming home at all. Nancy was at a loss as to what to do to help Ellen.

What frustration and sadness Nancy must have felt about Ellen's regression when she returned home! You already know some of the essentials that Nancy can use to help herself and Ellen. Let's step into a new essential: Engagement. As we describe below, you can work on attachment, attuning, and listening to improve engagement with your teen.

You may have heard of attachment and attachment theory. Attachment theory originated in the work of John Bowlby, a twentieth-century psychiatrist and psychoanalyst. This psychological, evolutionary, and ethological theory provides a descriptive and explanatory framework for understanding interpersonal relationships between people. Attachment theorists hold that children need a secure relationship with adult caregivers, and without such a relationship, normal social and emotional development will not occur.[1] As we talk about attachment in this chapter, we consider attachment to be an important part of a child's development.

Children naturally become attached to and move toward adults who are emotionally safe and present for them. Children move away from adults who are emotionally unsafe. As adults, we do the same. With this in mind, when engaging with our teen, it is of utmost importance to be in as safe of an emotional place as possible. In the past, when you were triggered by your teen's behavior, it's likely that you had a history of encounters with your teen that came from an unsafe place. Your presence may have been conditionally loving, controlling, angry, fearful, or judging. Your teen naturally moved away from you and toward peers or other adults who appeared to be safer for them.

It is heartbreaking to have your child move away from you. You as a parent desire a relationship and connection with your child. You can help your child in moving toward you by recognizing the importance and meaning of attachment and learning to recognize when your child is moving away from you. When your child does move away from you, ask yourself if you are offering your teen an emotionally safe place for engagement. Are you in some way asking your teen to fulfill your needs? Your continued practice in recognizing your own needs and developing healthy boundaries will allow you to provide these for yourself instead of asking your teen to provide them.

Along with attachment, learning to attune to your teen will help you to engage your teen. When your teen acts out, it is easy to lecture her about what you see as irresponsible, unhealthy, or destructive choices. It is easy to stand on the outside at a safe distance and judge her actions. But this stance, being on the outside, keeps a wall—built out of fear and your triggers—between you and your teen. Rather than standing on the outside, you can suspend judgment, enter into your child's world, and stand in her shoes. We call this "attuning."

Attuning is by definition entering into a harmonious or responsive relationship. It is a one-way process with you being sensitive and reflective regarding your teen's internal experience in the moment. In many ways, attuning is using your heart lens to view your teen. It is also being with your teen without any judgment. The following list shows how you view and engage your teen's behavior in two different ways, with and without attuning:

NOT ATTUNING · VIEWED BY MIND LENS	ATTUNING · VIEWED BY HEART LENS
DISRESPECTFUL BEHAVIOR	**DISTRESSFUL BEHAVIOR**
Want to control it	Comfort it
Stop it	Validate it
Punish it	Soothe it
Consequence it	Understand where it is coming from
Judge it	Meet it with compassion
DEFIANT BEHAVIOR	**FEARFUL BEHAVIOR**
Judge it	Create safety for it
Stop it	Be curious about it
Punish it	Listen to it
Consequence it	Hold it
Shame it	Validate it
Guilt it	Comfort it

When you are able to attune to your own emotional state and move toward your teen, understand what he is feeling and have compassion for his feelings, you are responding to where he is instead of wanting him to be someone else. In doing this, you will join with your teen rather than alienate him. Your teen will be able to move toward you and be more likely to ask for the love and support he needs. Attunement also allows you to trust your gut and be responsive to your teen without him even realizing it. As an example of attunement, consider the following story:

> When Eric picked up his son, Shane, from school, he could tell from Shane's body that he was in a bad mood and experiencing stress of some kind. Eric worked to calm himself as Shane put his seat belt on and just felt Shane's stress. Knowing Shane was usually hungry after school and liked to eat out, he said, "Hey Shane. Seems like you might have had a rough day. Can I take you to get something to eat?" Eric knew this wasn't the right time to discuss why Shane hadn't put his dishes away before they left for school that morning. He recognized that there would be a more productive time to have that conversation when Shane was less stressed.

When you are attuning to your child, be aware of judgments that may get in the way. These come in the form of interpretations of the behavior that may not be valid. In the example above, if Eric knew that Shane had a test at school, he wouldn't jump to the judgment that Shane was lazy and forgot to study. These judgments create a cascade of emotions that typically result in feelings of anger, resentment, and frustration. If judgments arise, take care of yourself before addressing your teen so that you have the emotional flexibility to attune to what your teen is experiencing.

As a parent, your job is not to be the judge in your teen's life. Such a role distances you from your teen, and he has plenty of people to take the role. Your job is to be a loving leader, someone your teen wants to connect with because he senses your unconditional love.

LISTENING

In a normal day, we hear many, many sounds. Some sounds we listen to and some sounds we are able to mentally turn off. Have you ever seen a baby sleep soundly while a vacuum is being run? As we discussed in Chapter 1: Awareness, our brains filter out sensory information. This ability can be helpful and harmful when it comes to listening. When interacting with your teen, you may not listen attentively, distracted by thoughts about other things or about what your teen is going to say or do next. If you are triggered in response to what you are hearing, you are especially susceptible to not listening. You know you're not listening well if your teen says, "You're not listening to me." Your teen is picking up that you are listening to something else—your inner thoughts.

To listen attentively to your teen, you must again practice suspending judgment and dealing with your triggers in order to fully hear your teen. Your task when you listen to your teen is to attune with her, enter her world, and validate her. Whether you agree with what she is saying is not important. Regardless of your thoughts, what she is expressing is her reality. And your teen wants to know that you can see her reality. You are helping to fulfill her need to be seen, heard, and validated.

When you are fully listening, you also give your teen the space to express all that she has to say. You give her the time she needs without cutting her off or jumping in. You may have to handle your emotions and triggers to do this and also delay your needs. Your teen may be ready to talk at inconvenient times—when you are rushing off to work or trying to go to bed. Giving your teen the time and presence in which to talk will send your teen the message, "You are vitally important. Your experience and emotions are valid. I see you." When you listen to your thoughts about what the future might bring or what your child's past was, you are making the listening all about you, rather than your child. Attentive listening will go a long way in keeping the engagement a loving one.

As you begin to engage more and more with your child from a heart-centered place, in a way that lacks an agenda, you will have the opportunity to learn more and more about your teen. Attachment, attuning, and listening will enhance the engaging interactions you have and build a platform on which the both of you meet with equally important needs. To illustrate what we have learned about engagement, let's look back at the story about Ellen and Nancy in which Nancy changes how she interacts with Ellen:

At a loss as to how to connect with her daughter, Nancy began working on awareness and self-care until she could provide an unconditionally loving presence to her daughter Ellen. When she was ready, she set dates for tea with her daughter at a local restaurant. Ellen came to each date, and at each one, Nancy surrendered her agenda and beliefs about how Ellen should be behaving. After awhile, the dates for tea became dates for dinner. One night, Ellen went home to have dinner with Nancy. They were sitting in the living room after dinner, and Ellen had curled up under a blanket. She became comfortable and opened up to her mom about her fears about the future and how much she disliked herself. The more she opened up, the further she went under the blanket until she was hiding. Attuning and listening, Nancy moved toward Ellen, put a hand on her arm and said, "You know, I wasn't there for you. I wasn't able to be because I was too scared. But I'm here now. What can I take from you?" She paused. "Can I hold your blanket for you now? I'm ready. I can do it now. I couldn't do it then." Ellen took off the blanket and handed it to her mom, and her mom continued, "I'm here now. You can give it all to me, and I'll hold it."

You may experience some of the common challenges to engaging with your teen, including guilt about attachment with your child, unmet physical needs, a lack of desire to engage with your child, and attachment with adopted children.

Depending on your past with your teen, your teen may not have developed attachment to you as a child and now as a teen. Children are wonderfully resilient and their attachment to you can change. As you continue your work to take care of yourself and to create relational safety with your child, you become the safe place she can attach to. If you have guilt over poor attachment with your child, this is a good time to work with your guilt, heal old wounds, and to move through it. You did the best you could do at the time with what you had. Celebrate that you are making strides toward changing your relationship with your child.

Physical needs can present challenges to engaging with your child. If you are tired, hungry, thirsty, or sick, you will not be as present or as good at attuning and listening to your child because your body has your attention. Take care of those physical needs that you can in the moment—have a snack or drink water—and verbalize to your child where you are. You can say something like, "Honey, I will do my best to listen to you right now, but just know that I'm a little off because I'm tired/not feeling well. But I do want to hear what you are saying." If you are feeling a little "off" and need help identifying what you need, use the Wellness Check in Chapter 1: Awareness.

Another challenge can be a lack of desire to engage with your teen. This lack of desire may arise from your physical needs or emotional needs, from being distracted by the beliefs you've built around his actions, from not "liking" your child at the moment, or from the fear of what may feel like a confrontation. When you are having trouble engaging with your child, take care of your own physical and emotional needs, use a support person to bring you back to a more present place, practice gratitude for your child, and remember to come from a place of curiosity and not from judgment as you engage with your child.

Likewise, your child will have times when he does not want to engage with you. Do not force engagement. Give your teen the space he needs and remember that he is taking care of his needs to be better able to engage with you. You can use the energy you have for engagement to expand your presence, to give your teen, wherever he is, the sense that you are an unconditionally loving place.

Attachment issues may be more at the forefront for adopted teens, who may be dealing with traumas experienced before their adoption. For adopted teens, it is critical for parents to create a safe emotional container for them to work through their original traumas. Often the way children deal with the trauma of abandonment is to create limiting beliefs that they are unworthy of love and that others aren't dependable enough to open up to. Even though they may be desperate to love, they have big barriers and need time and a loving presence to make them feel safe enough to attach. On the part of parents, parents sometimes have been through years of wanting a child, dealing with infertility issues and feelings of inadequacy. They can also have high expectations for themselves and their adopted child to instantly bond and connect in a loving way. In the dance of balancing all of your needs, if your need to be loved is stronger than your child's need to feel safe, you may take her defensive stance personally. You may inadvertently withdraw your love due to your belief that your child should love you the way you imagine he should. Withdrawing love then exacerbates his fear of being abandoned.

Remember to use the essentials you have learned when being with your adoptive child. Heart-centered parenting creates a safe environment where your child's traumas can be worked through and resolved. If you feel the need for outside support, seek those who understand and work with attachment issues through a heart-centered model.

KEY LEARNINGS

- Engagement is choosing to join together—to connect—while recognizing that both parties have equal needs.
- Engagement is connecting without a power struggle.
- Dealing with your own triggers and needs are key to engaging with your child.
- You can enhance your engagement with your child through attachment, attuning, and listening.

PERSONAL PRACTICES

1. Listen to yourself, setting aside all fear, shame, and judgment, and listening to your heart with love. Ask yourself, what are my needs right now?

2. Practice listening with a partner, friend, or your teen. Take two minutes and listen attentively to without letting your mind jump to anything else. Then take five, ten, twenty minutes to really listen. When you have the opportunity to listen to your teen, imagine taking off your conventional parenting ears, those ears that listen to the limiting beliefs you have about your teen. Really let go of everything and get curious about the message your teen is giving you through her words or behavior. If fears come up for you, track those stories and later bring your awareness to them.

3. The following sample dialogue may be helpful in learning how to help your teen open up and talk while you are listening:

Teen: "Mom, you have been such a jerk lately. You are so preoccupied with how everyone sees you and the image of our family."

Mom: "Wow, Chelsea, you are really upset with me. Thank you for telling me. I thought something was upsetting you. I'd love to hear more about your experience if you want to share." (Remember the conversation is about your relationship, not whether you have been a jerk. It can be hard to stay open at this point, because your child is attacking you and accusing you. Try not to focus on the details and follow your child's lead. Be a safe emotional space, and your child will open up and speak.)

Teen: "Well, I hated it when you asked me in front of your friends if I was going to shower, implying that I 'should' shower. And you didn't even notice that I had been crying."

Mom: "Sounds like I really missed seeing you and how you were feeling."

Teen: "Yeah, you did. I was so upset and all you seemed to care about was whether I looked presentable to your friends, but I was really sad."

Mom: "Sounds like you knew how to take care of yourself by ignoring me and my friends and hanging out in your room on the phone all night. Do you want to tell me what happened?"

Teen: "I just feel so much pressure to look a certain way. And I had been out with Megan and Emily, and they were both bragging about how they'd been losing all this weight, and you know I have been working really hard to just accept my body how it is, and then I come home after I already felt like horrible, and get the message from you that I really don't look good."

Mom: (Just nod and listen)

Teen: "What I really needed was for you to hug me."

Mom: "Instead what I did was criticize you, huh?"

4. The following dialogue may be helpful in learning how to validate your teen even when you disagree with him:

Teen: "I hate it when you try to control me. You don't love me. You just want to control what I do. You suck as a dad."

Dad: "You are really angry that I said no to giving you that money, aren't you? Tell me more about it."

Teen: "Oh, shut up, you don't really want to hear me."

Dad: "I know Nick, that is how it has been in the past, but I really do want to hear about how angry that makes you."

Teen: "Yeah, right, so you can blame me later for being selfish and greedy?"

Dad: "Nick, I can hear how angry you are that I have misunderstood you and lashed out at you when I didn't understand what you were asking for."

Teen: "You always gripe about how entitled I am and that I never do anything around the house to help you. It's all about how bad I am."

Dad: "That's true, I have said that to you in the past, and I'm really sorry. When I get stressed, I'm realizing I 'act out' too. It must have been really hard for you when I was blaming you for not helping. I was telling you that you were selfish, and I can see now that this wasn't true."

Teen: "Yeah, I just want to have fun, and you always ask me to do things around the house when you want them done. You never seem to notice that I'm doing something that I want to do."

Dad: "Nick, thank you for letting me know how it really is for you. I can see that I haven't been respecting you and taking into account where you are before asking for help. I really hear you and am working on changing my part in this. Thanks for letting me know."

Teen: "Hey Dad, by the way can I have the money?"

Dad: "No, Nick. And remember, I love you."

5. When you are with your teen, whatever state she is in, do your best to calm yourself. Place aside your thoughts and judgments about what she is experiencing and why. Focus on feeling her experience from a caring place. This practice can help you attune to your teen.

"Out beyond ideas of wrongdoing and rightdoing, there is a field. I will meet you there."

RUMI

6

GUIDANCE

guid·ance *(noun)*: the act or process of guiding; a mindful dance with another person of knowing and not knowing and of sharing and listening.

As you become an emotionally safe place for your teen and offer the kind of presence that she wants to move toward, you will have the opportunity to be close enough to your teen that you can begin offering guidance. In this chapter, we will discuss and describe the essential of guidance and working on another part of being a loving leader—offering guidance.

We discussed the power of parents in the Introduction and want to remind you again that your teen needs you. As you may have suspected, teens make decisions in different ways than adults. This is more than a function of hormones or increasing independence, disrespect, or disobedience. Biologically, your teen's frontal lobes, where the faculties of planning and reasoning are centered, are still developing. Teens tend to use the amygdala that guides instinctual or "gut" reactions to make decisions. As a result, a teen's decisions appear more impulsive or even dangerous because they come from a place of gut reaction.[1] Your teen is not merely acting out but still developing physically. Your teen still needs you to provide guidance for, but not control over, his decisions.

In parenting, we often hear about parents "raising" their kids. Rather than raising your teen, we are going to ask you to offer guidance to your teen. Raising a child indicates that you have an image of what you want your teen to look like, a kind of template, and you are moving your child (raising him) into that image. Raising a child can have many negative consequences, because the parent is trying to control his child and mold him into a specific form, according to the parent's agenda and needs. In contrast, when parents offer guidance, the child may not follow the guidance—but she can express herself, learn how to interact with others in a loving way, and grow into her own image of herself with the loving support of parents who are there when she shares her life.

To give you a picture of what raising versus guiding means, read the following story:

> As Paul, the oldest of five children, was growing up, his parents had strict rules about most areas of his life. His parents decided what he and his siblings could wear, how they could have their hair cut, what books they could read, what music they could listen to, which

movies they could see, what subjects they studied in school, when and what they ate for dinner, where they took vacations, how many and what sports and musical instruments each child could play, and what career they expected their children to enter. For Paul, his father made it clear that Paul was to go to college, get a good-paying job in business, and earn enough money to support other family members if they needed his help.

When Paul was in college and his youngest two siblings were still at home, his youngest brother was convicted of shoplifting. Paul's parents realized that they needed to do something different, and so began practicing heart-centered parenting. Paul saw a dramatic shift in how his parents related to him and how they related to his younger siblings. His parents started asking their children their opinions on clothes, meals, vacations, school subjects, and extracurricular activities. In Paul's sophomore year of college, his father called him and told him about his shift in parenting. He said, "Paul, I'm curious about something. What do you want to study in college?" Paul replied that he'd always wanted to do more writing. His dad, who in the past mocked him for thinking about any other career than business and hammered the importance of making money, replied, "Really. I didn't know that. What kind of writing?"

Your practice with the *Chaos to Connection* essentials is bringing you to a place, like Paul's parents, where you can begin to offer guidance to her, supporting her as she matures into who she is, being curious about her inner inclinations, and modeling connected relationships so she can have them with you and other people. All children need to have the opportunity to take chances and to find their way in the world. Teens often know their own limits as to what they can do. They can find their way if you are a guide.

Offering guidance to your teen can be a delicate affair. You don't want to lecture or nag, nor do you want to avoid providing wisdom and learning opportunities for him. You also want to find the right time when your teen is receptive and not assume that you know what is best for your child. We will discuss below how to offer guidance through experience, wisdom, and confidence.

EXPERIENCE

As an adult, you have many experiences that make up your past and have led you to places of growth, insight, and wisdom. Leaving wisdom aside for the moment, it is important as you consider your life experiences to realize that your teen is creating her own experiences. You may have truly wonderful experiences that you want your teen to also have, but it is important to follow your teen's lead on what experiences you guide her toward. Depending on differences between you and your teen, an experience that you cherished may be torture to your teen. For example, you may love going to football games, but your teen would rather spend time at a music concert. You may have loved your college experience at a small, private liberal arts college, but your teen wants to go to a large state university. Expecting your teen to enjoy what you enjoy or to follow in your footsteps often backfires. Allowing your teen to have different experiences than you gives her room to have her own experiences and discover herself in the world.

With that said, you may have the opportunity to share your experiences with your teen. By attuning to your teen and his readiness, you will know when you can share with him experiences you enjoy. You may even find that your teen is curious about you and your past experiences, even as he experiences them differently. Sharing your experiences with your teen is a way to deepen your relationship, as long as the expectation is not for him to have the same.

WISDOM

Your life experiences inform you about the world and about being a teenager, providing you with insight and wisdom that you've learned along the way. Parents often err on two extremes—providing too much or too little wisdom. When you are guiding your child, remember that it can be a tricky balance between nagging and neglecting to share. Timing is key when sharing your wisdom. By attuning with and listening to your teen, you can learn the best time to share your wisdom. If you and your teen are having a great conversation, and she starts to have a "glazed over" look, then it is time to stop sharing your wisdom. Likewise, if your teen is upset—venting, raging, crying—the moment to share your wisdom is at a later time. In fact, when we are in stress mode our brain cannot process or really use shared wisdom. Your teen's brain will be better receptive at a later time, once she has calmed down. Of course, if your teen asks for your advice, this is a great time to share your wisdom.

Often, parents forget to tap into this wisdom for a variety of reasons—lack of confidence, fear of "being a good parent," or fear of disclosing too much. Your experiences of being misunderstood, being told what to do, and being controlled by forces outside of you are powerful places from which to share wisdom with your child. When you suspend your fear and your need to be in charge, you open the door to sharing wisdom with your teen, joining him and understanding where he is coming from.

Remember again that your teen will continue to pursue her own experiences and to develop her own wisdom. You may offer sage advice and priceless wisdom, which your teen does not follow. Offering guidance to your teen is to fulfill your teen's need, not yours. Whether or not your teen follows your wisdom is not as important as you continuing to be a loving leader to your teen.

Confidence—in a variety of areas—is important to guiding your child. We find that many teens we work with lack the confidence that they can be who they want to be without letting their parents down. The expectations parents place on them and the withdrawing of love based on their behavior tear down the innate confidence they carry when they are young.

You can build your child's confidence by being confident yourself in how you are present for your child. Having the confidence to show up for your teen in whatever way she needs allows her to feel safe and to know you are there for her. Having the confidence to "not know" what is best for your child, using your curiosity with your teen, can also help her become more self-confident. Indeed, having the confidence to know that your teen will survive if you stop teaching and just love her where she is requires the ultimate confidence.

You are already practicing the steps to improve your and your child's confidence through growing your awareness, presence, and engagement. Continue to be present and to engage with your child's heart, using your own experience, wisdom, and confidence, and you will support him in building his own confidence.

Now that we have looked at how and when to make use of your experience and wisdom and the importance of confidence, let's look at another story about parents who changed from raising to guiding their child:

When Megan was a sophomore in high school, she started to get lower and lower grades, to use marijuana, and to date several boys at once. Megan's parents became aware that Megan was having problems in school early on, and they responded by grounding her and restricting her from playing soccer until her grades improved. Over and over again, Megan's dad lectured her on the importance of school, getting a job, and being able to support herself. He said to her one night, "When you turn eighteen, you can get a job, go to college, or join the military, but we're not supporting you." Megan soon flunked out of school, began selling drugs, being sexually promiscuous, and spending very little time at home.

Megan's parents began practicing heart-centered parenting. Instead of focusing on motivating Megan to get her life together and meet their expectations, they began focusing on their reactions to Megan's behaviors. They became aware of their feelings, began creating emotional safety, and got the support they needed to surrender their agendas for Megan. They began to provide an unconditionally loving presence from which to engage Megan.

At first, Megan pushed even harder, letting her parents know how little she wanted or needed their guidance in her life. She made it clear that she could take care of herself. When her parents began to validate how courageous Megan was for following her desire for freedom, she began to become curious as to what was going on. She was used to her parents lecturing her and showing their intense disappointment in her. At first, she was suspicious that they were manipulating her to conform to their image of her. And yet, as they continued to show up, without their agendas, Megan began opening to the possibility that they might be willing to understand her needs and even support her choices.

Over time, Megan began to ask her parents for support and even began to illicit their guidance in how to find a school on-line to finish her degree. She began to open up to her mother about her relationships with boys, and as her mother continued to see her from her heart lens instead of judging her behavior, Megan began to seek more and more guidance and wisdom from both parents.

Such a transformation in Megan—and her parents—sounds like magic. It's not. Such a transformation is made possible by parents who practice the essentials of heart-centered parenting to provide a loving presence and become loving leaders, providing guidance to their child rather than mandating change.

You may experience some of the common challenges other parents experience in providing guidance to your teen, including concern about your child's motivation, changing your leadership role, derailing your child's emotional cycle with wisdom, and handling positive triggers.

One of the most common challenges we see in parents as they learn about heart-centered parenting is a fear that their child will never learn motivation if they drop their agenda. Internal motivation, however, comes from being seen, accepted, and feeling love. When a parent tries to drive their child to motivation through constant external motivation—through rules, threats, or rewards—the child will not develop internal motivation. For the teen, external motivations feel like withdrawing of love and intense pushing from the parents. In under-motivated teens, when parents change their focus to loving their teen and holding him right where he is, the teen has the opportunity to find the calm and peace in which he can develop emotionally and find his own motivation.

In heart-centered parenting, parents, especially fathers, may find it very difficult to change their traditional driving parental role with their teen. If you find it difficult to shift to guiding, you can be confident that, given the right space, your teen will know what is best for her. You can explain what worked for you, but without the expectation that your teen will necessarily follow your example. And be confident that it's important to share at the right moment even if your teen does not follow the wisdom. Remember that when it comes down to it, you don't have control over your child's behavior. If you feel like you are giving up control, this is an indication that you are trying hard to control.

As mentioned in the section on wisdom, knowing the right time to share experiences and wisdom can be a challenge. Without question, when your child is experiencing an intense feeling and moving through the emotional cycle, the only thing you can effectively provide is a loving presence in which to hold her. Sharing experience and wisdom can become a way to derail your child from completing the emotional cycle. It is better to wait until your child has gone through the emotional cycle and come to a state where she is receptive to your experience and wisdom. This may be soon after the intense experience, or it may be the next day. As you become more attuned to your child, you will get a sense of when she is receptive to you.

A final common challenge is positive triggers. As you engage more and more with your child, you may be positively triggered by your teen. You may want to praise your teen's behavior because you feel better based on his behavior. Like negative triggers, positive triggers are the result of your beliefs, judgments, and needs. Positive triggers are as problematic as negative triggers if your teen changes his behavior to please you. You again give your teen power over your emotions. Practice with your positive triggers as you do with negative ones, being curious about what needs are behind such triggers. They may be the same as your negative ones. Do acknowledge your teen, but for those things that give your teen pleasure, not necessarily what gives you pleasure.

KEY LEARNINGS

- Guiding your child is much more effective and loving than raising her.
- Your experiences are important and valid but will differ from your teen's experiences.
- Your wisdom is also important and worth sharing with your teen.
- Drop your expectations that your teen will experience things as you did or that she will follow your wisdom.
- Have confidence that you can show up for your teen and that you don't always know what is best for your teen.

PERSONAL PRACTICES

1. Imagine being a "guide on the side" rather than a "sage on the stage" persona. The sage on the stage lectures or talks down to her audience. Imagine you are guiding from the side, shoulder-to-shoulder, rather than "nose-to-nose" issuing orders.

2. Think about a place to meet with your teen that you know she likes and that is on common ground. Decide how long you can be with your teen before you start to lecture. Set a date with your teen to meet at that place for that amount of time. If you start with five minutes, start there! As you get better at showing up, increase how much time you spend with your teen.

3. Go for a nice long drive with your teen. Spend a lot of time listening as he opens up, and wait for openings to offer your input or opinion. The key is to provide a loving presence and enough listening and safety so that even if there is no opportunity for guidance, your teen will feel comfortable reaching out to you when they need support. Driving in the car provides a safe environment to begin conversations because you are both strapped in and sitting side by side.

4. Find an activity that is new to both you and your teen. Let your teen lead, and you follow. Be curious and watch how your teen learns and how you learn.

5. Practice how to respond when your teen asks for advice. If your teen asks, "What should I do?" Tell him the truth, "I don't know, honey. I can't know what's best for you. This is what I did in a similar situation, and it worked for me. Whatever decision you make, you can know that I'm always here to listen and that I'm always going to love you. You'll know what to do."[1]

"We cannot teach people anything; we can only help them discover it within themselves."

III

thri·ving *(verb)*: growing vigorously; flourishing; growing together with forgiveness, perseverance, gratitude, and vision.

As you continue what you have learned in Surviving and Reviving, growing your awareness, engaging with each other, and providing relational and emotional safety, you come to a place where everyone is well enough to begin growing, flourishing, having fun together, and thriving. Take a moment again to feel gratitude for yourself for all that you have done for yourself, your child, and your family. You are beginning to create a family with a culture of awareness, curiosity, self-knowing, and unconditional love to meet each member where she is in the moment. You are continuing to make the changes that will move you from chaos to connection.

We continue with the nine heart-centered parenting essentials of *Chaos to Connection* in Thriving, a mode in which you and your family have survived the emergency room and revived your relationships. The focus is now on "us"—you and your child together. This is a new image of your family!

The next three heart-centered essentials are found in Thriving. You may be wondering how to know if your practice is really working and if you are moving from Reviving into Thriving. The following comparison of the characteristics of Reviving with characteristics of Thriving will show you the progress you are making.

REVIVING	THRIVING
Improved ability to handle high stress even as the intensity in your family may build.	Continuing ability to handle new stress (you and your teen).
	Experiencing less stress and more joy.
Stopping, sitting, and breathing.	Constantly embracing the moment and focusing less on right and wrong.
Creating a gap.	Watching and embracing your feelings without letting them control your actions.
Realizing, "I am not the feelings. I am separate from the experience itself."	
Taking care of yourself and doing wellness checks.	Taking care of yourself and doing wellness checks (you and your teen).
Feeling less out of control, regaining personal power.	Setting and keeping internal boundaries (you and your teen).
Feeling more confident, grounded, and ready to meet new challenges.	Feeling seen, heard, and validated (you and your teen).
Feeling like you're moving.	
Dropping judgment and increasing curiosity about yourself and your teen.	Continuing curiosity about yourself and your teen and from your teen about you.
Connecting to physical sensations to notice triggers and stress.	Having emotional intimacy with yourself, your teen, and others in your life.
Sometimes looking at yourself from the outside and naming what's really going on.	Able to see yourself when you are surviving but acknowledging it and moving on.
Starting to notice yourself and being aware of your emotional reactivity.	Seeing emotional maturity in yourself & your teen, who may tell you when you are surviving.
Working with your emotions in a more positive way with awareness, support and safety.	
Starting to enjoy being in your home.	Focusing on maintaining yourself.
Focusing on yourself even as your teen does not change his acting out behavior.	Enjoying being with your child, engaging, and guiding.
	Feeling a sense of "we" in your family.
	Less fighting, acting out and more playfulness in your family.
Using your heart lens and increasing emotional safety.	Able to go through your emotional cycles (you and your teen).
	Ability to be there for your teen when she is going through emotional cycles.
	Having emotional resiliency (you and your teen).
	Confidently providing safety and support in your family.
Feeling like you're in foreign territory & in transition as you practice unconditional love.	Having compassion for yourself and your teen and your teen having compassion for you.
	Knowing that things shift & you can always return to a place of calm & unconditional love.
Questioning yourself and doubting the *Chaos to Connection* process.	Feeling confidence in the *Chaos to Connection* process.
	Wanting to share *Chaos to Connection* with other parents.

As you read through the characteristics, you may notice how much longer and more meaningful the characteristics of Thriving are. Whereas your child is the focus when you are reviving, you and your child (a "we") become the focus when you are thriving. When you are thriving, you are on a whole new level of relationship with your child and those around you. Your inner self, your emotions, and those of others around you are being seen, heard, and validated. You connect, strengthen, and play with each other. Your relationship with your teen has new levels of complexity and layers. You see your child's behavior, which you used to see as disrespectful, defiant, lazy, or dishonest, as a communication that you need to be present and truly to listen. You see her behavior as a call for love, and a need for support and emotional safety.

While thriving is where you want to live with your family, you will continue for the rest of your life to move in and out of Surviving, Reviving, and Thriving. This is living! You are at a point where you can recognize those other modes and use your new skills to move through them.

In this third section, we will define, discuss, illustrate, and provide practices for the three Thriving essentials: **Forgiveness, Perseverance,** and **Vision.**

"The phoenix hope, can wing her way through the desert skies, and still defying fortune's spite; revive from ashes and rise."

MIGUEL DE CERVANTES

7

FORGIVENESS

for·give·ness *(noun)*: the act of forgiving; allowing room for error or weakness; giving up resentment of or claim to requital for; ceasing to feel resentment against an offender; the act of pardoning yourself and others.

You have been on an incredible journey in the first six chapters of *Chaos to Connection*, turning your awareness to yourself and then turning to engage your teen. We know that you have found within you the ability and love to move toward unconditionally loving yourself and your teen. You are moving into a state of being that allows you and your teen to grow individually and together as "we" and "us."

As you have grown in unconditional love, you have likely practiced forgiveness. Ongoing forgiveness is so important that it's an essential unto itself and necessary for thriving. People often refer to a refusal to forgive as "carrying a grudge." Indeed, choosing not to forgive, or choosing not to apologize, is like picking up a heavy burden and carrying it everywhere. Without forgiveness, we experience diminished self-love and damaged self-esteem. We will first reframe forgiveness and then discuss how removing judgment and increasing gratitude and empathy deepen forgiveness.

Forgiveness is often viewed as something you do for another person. The reality is, the emotions you feel about someone or someone's actions are living inside of you and causing you pain, not the other person. Forgiveness, then, is not something you do for another person but an act you do for yourself to bring yourself greater peace and happiness. Forgiveness does not condone the other person's behavior or the hurt that happens, but forgiveness frees you from continuing to live in the old pain and suffering, releasing you to live more freely in the present moment.

Consider the following story before the father is able to practice forgiveness:

Will came home late one night, stumbling and unable to speak clearly. It was clear to Dan, Will's father, that Will was drunk. Standing in the living room with Will, Dan felt a wave of fear and disgust as he thought about his own alcoholism. He yelled at Will, "What were you thinking? Where have you been? You're so drunk I can smell you from ten feet away. You can forget about going out any time in the next two months. There's no way you're going to prom at the end of the year. Don't even think about it." Will tried to protest, but Dan yelled back, "I don't want to hear another word from you! Get out of my sight!"

Like Dan, your history and beliefs color how you view your teen's actions and place judgment where judgment isn't needed. Your true self—free from triggers, limiting beliefs, neediness—is unable to be with your child unless you forgive. Through forgiveness of yourself, you can come to a place where you forgive yourself for your history and beliefs. In this space, your relationship with your teen continues to move beyond taking care of you to a strong relationship in which you unconditionally love your teen and want to continue to grow in that relationship.

You may feel that you need to forgive your teen for her behavior or for how her behavior has hurt you. In fact, it is you that you need to forgive for the judgments you make about your teen's behavior. As we've described previously, your teen's emotional response or behavioral choices are always appropriate based on how she interprets her situation. Whether the behavior is right or wrong is not inherent in the behavior but comes from your judgment. When this is seen—that your teen is doing the best she can in the moment—nothing needs to be forgiven. But if you judge your teen as wrong or bad, then forgiveness of yourself for your judgment is necessary. In other words, forgiveness releases us from our wrongdoings. If there is no wrongdoing, no release is needed.

REMOVING JUDGMENT

Judgments, placing a right and wrong label on emotions or behaviors, are barriers to loving yourself and to a loving relationship with your child, as we saw in the last six chapters. By their nature, judgments separate you from your authentic self because they unite how you behave and the results you create with who you are. Your judgments about your teen, then, also prevent you from seeing who she truly is, and you see her behavior as who she is. Seeing only your teen's behavior prevents you from moving toward your child to find out what is behind her behavior and to know her authentic self. This separation from the true self causes pain and distance from others. When you release your judgments, you set yourself free from the limitations your thinking imposes on yourself and others.

The good news is that judgments, though powerful, can be removed once they are identified. You release judgments through some of the essentials you have already learned—awareness, presence, and engagement. By practicing these essentials you are moving beyond judgments of right and wrong and removing limiting beliefs so that you can be in the present moment.

You can also practice and choose to think differently through forgiveness. A simple way to grow in this area is to use the statement, "I forgive myself for judging myself as …" or "I forgive myself for judging [insert name] as …" Typically, you will find that you make judgments toward yourself or others based on aspects of yourself that you do not like or that scare you. These are parts that you do not want to own. Using the statement above, you might tell yourself, "I forgive myself for judging myself as a bad mother" or "I forgive myself for judging myself as unworthy" or "I forgive myself for judging my child as disrespectful." You may need time for true forgiveness and a change in your judgments to occur. Give yourself this time.

You will find as you release judgments about yourself and your teen that you do not need to forgive your teen. But you may find that you want to apologize to your teen and ask for your teen's forgiveness. The best apology is honest and comes from a position of presence and unconditional love, not neediness or with expectations. For example, apologizing with "I was a complete idiot. I don't know what I was thinking" is not as sincere or unconditionally loving as "I was just trying to look out for you because I am scared. But, looking back, I know I need to take care of my own emotions and not ask you to make me feel safe. I'm sorry. I love you." Your apology is your process of forgiveness. Your teen, because she is not responsible for your emotions nor are you for hers, will have her own emotional response, possibly forgiveness but possibly anger. Through your process of an apology, you show your teen that, like her, you were doing the best you could with what you had at the moment, and you are growing in unconditional love.

GRATITUDE

As you are working to release judgments, gratitude toward your teen can move you toward forgiveness and free you from the burden of holding on to old hurts. By definition, gratitude is a state of being grateful, appreciative, or thankful. Gratitude involves appreciating both the good and the bad and adopting the attitude that the present moment, whatever it looks like, is a gift.

You can practice gratitude throughout your regular day. For instance, when your child ignores you when you ask him to do chores, and you hear yourself nagging and shaming him, take a moment and notice you can be thankful your child is at home and still there for you to love. Instead of focusing on the chores, focus on your gratitude for who he is, not what he is doing or not doing. Give gratitude for him showing you where your focus is. This isn't to shame yourself for your needs but to see the true situation. Real gratitude begins as appreciation for what is, instead of saving your gratitude until your child meets your behavioral expectations.

With gratitude you can see that children are an amazing gift, in joyful *and* challenging times. In the challenging times, your teen provides you with an opportunity, through your triggers, to discover places of hurt and limiting belief and for you to find healing and to release those beliefs. For past, current, and future challenging times with your teen, acknowledge gratitude for the gift your teen has given you: the opportunity to learn and grow. From this perspective, whatever your outside experience is, it is valuable and made more so by your teen. Your teen's behavior is in service to letting go of your limiting beliefs.

While practicing gratitude, be mindful of the shadow side of gratitude. The shadow side of gratitude is the self-defeating voice that says you should be grateful for what you have instead of complaining. True gratitude is a call to be where you are without basing your happiness on your child's actions toward you. This idea of gratitude is evident in the origin of the word "gratitude." "Gratitude" and "grace" share a common origin, the Latin word "gratus," meaning "pleasing" or "thankful." When experiencing a true state of gratitude, you will often feel the power and presence of grace.

EMPATHY

Like gratitude, empathy can move you toward forgiveness. Empathy is heart-centered, felt from the heart rather than thought from the mind. Unlike sympathy, when you are empathetic, you do not judge what is happening as an outsider but attune to your teen and feel what your teen is feeling. With empathy, you respect your teen and the dignity of the journey she is on. You have likely experienced empathy many times in your child's life. You have empathy when your child is hurting—physically or emotionally—and you often vicariously experience what your child is feeling, thinking, and experiencing. You may feel empathy with your child to such a point that you cry or rage with him. In times of joy, you feel empathy to such an extent that you laugh and celebrate with him.

Having empathy for your teen provides you with the opportunity to be an emotionally safe place of unconditional love. In unconditional love, you again do not judge your teen but hold her without needing to rescue yourself or your teen. You are in a place where you move beyond forgiveness because you have removed your judgment. For example, if your teen expresses herself by yelling at you, you can have empathy for her strong, angry feeling and use that empathy to enter into curiosity about her. You understand that your teen's emotional state and behavior are about her, and you don't take them personally. In this way, empathy helps you to honor your teen's growth as an individual and provides you with greater understanding of your teen's own learning process and journey. When you have empathy for your teen, you connect with her and see who she is and what she is feeling, however she chooses to express herself in that moment.

You have learned about what forgiveness is, how to deepen it, and the importance of forgiveness. Keeping what you have learned in mind, let's return to the story of Dan and his son Will.

The morning after Will came home drunk, and Dan yelled at him, Dan was in the kitchen making coffee while Will was sleeping. He had laid awake most of the night thinking about Will, drunk in the living room. Dan thought back to when he had been drinking and all the years of recovery he had behind him. As he sat with this thought, he realized his reaction was about his own history and not about Will's drinking. Dan felt ashamed of his own alcoholism. He was scared that Will would become an alcoholic. Dan forgave himself that morning for being an alcoholic and for judging Will's behavior. As a result, Dan came to a place where he could love himself despite his alcoholism and judgments.

When Will got up, Dan poured him a cup of strong coffee and apologized for yelling. "You know, Will," he said, "I was really angry last night. And I realized this morning that my anger is toward myself and my own drinking, not you. I love you so much, and when I smelled the alcohol on your breath, I got triggered and projected into the future and my fear that you might be like me. I wasn't there for you, son, and I'm sorry. Can we try again?"

You will find as your forgiveness grows through removing judgment, practicing gratitude, and experiencing empathy that you grow in intimacy with your teen. Like Dan, as you put down the burden you are carrying, the load of past hurts and judgments, you free yourself and your teen to be with one another in an unconditionally loving relationship. Such forgiveness of yourself will move you to a place of joy for your life, for your teen, and for your family.

One more note about forgiveness. In all the work that you are doing, you are paving the way for others to follow your example. You may have other children that need to find healing in their relationship with their sibling that has been acting out. This is wonderful! You can best support your children in healing their relationship by letting go of your own agenda for such healing (you can't force healing), modeling a relationship with your children, and having unconditional love. Providing a space where each child feels seen, heard, and validated paves the way to forgiveness.

COMMON CHALLENGES

Forgiveness can present a number of challenges, especially as you are just beginning to practice forgiveness. You may find that removing judgments, being vulnerable, and having empathy take work and practice.

If you find that removing judgments is a challenge, give yourself time to work through your beliefs and emotions. It may be helpful to return to Chapter 1: Awareness and to use the practices to grow in awareness and taking care of yourself. Your judgments come from underlying beliefs that grow out of your experience. These beliefs and judgments are not set in stone. Remember, you can choose if you will live through them or not.

Forgiveness, gratitude, and empathy ask that you are vulnerable with yourself and with other people as you lay before yourself and others those beliefs and emotions that are in your heart. If you struggle with being vulnerable, read again the section on Vulnerability in Chapter 3: Support to increase your comfort level with vulnerability. Remember also that the love you grow for yourself allows you to hold internal boundaries with yourself and with others so that you have the capacity to experience vulnerability and connection. Self-love is the primary loving act that allows you to be unconditionally loving with others because you have taken care of yourself first.

Lastly, having empathy for your teen who has appeared to be the cause of stress and pain in your life can be a challenge. The following will help you move toward greater empathy: continuing to practice awareness; taking responsibility for your emotions; fulfilling your needs regardless of your child's behavior; remembering that your child's behavior is exactly as it should be in the moment and that your child, too, is learning. You can also try expressing the following, mentally or verbally, "Out of empathy I respect you, and the dignity of the journey you are on. I honor your growth as an individual. I value your learning process. I recognize that we are all doing our best to grow in our awareness of who we truly are. I am okay. You are okay. Your feelings are okay. I love you no matter what."

KEY LEARNINGS

- You do not forgive for the sake of the other person. You forgive for yourself.
- As you remove judgments about your child's behavior, you move beyond the need to forgive because there is no wrongdoing to forgive.
- Gratitude for the gift your teen has given you, the opportunity to learn and grow, can help you grow in forgiveness.
- Empathy for your child can remove your judgments and allow for forgiveness.
- Forgiveness unburdens you and makes room for connection.

PERSONAL PRACTICES

1. Mind dump—say out loud to yourself or a friend or write down—all judgments you make toward your child. For each judgment, forgive yourself for the judgment, recognizing that at your teen's core, she is worthy and loveable no matter what her outer expressions may be.

2. Use phrases like the following to practice forgiveness: "The truth is I am doing the best that I can. I am worthy. I am good enough. I am simply learning, and it is okay to be learning. I do not need to be perfect in order to be good enough. I am good enough. I am loveable. And my child is doing the best that he can. He gets angry when he is hurt. It is not personal. I did the best I could. He was simply doing the best that he could in that moment. Just as I was."

3. Think of something or someone you are not happy with. It might be getting a speeding ticket, your child's defiant behavior, or an unreasonable colleague at work. Now, find as many things as possible to be grateful for in the situation—a minimum of five. Notice as you are grateful for the situation what gifts the situation has given you.

4. Once a week, write out what you are thankful for in yourself and in your teen. This might be difficult at first, but start somewhere with something (i.e. I am grateful she came home last night. I am grateful he said 'Hi' to me today. I am grateful for this opportunity to love her). Share this with your teen.

"Forgiveness is choosing to love. It is the first skill of self-giving love."

GHANDI

8

PERSEVERANCE

per·se·ver·ance *(noun)*: the action or condition of persisting in a state, enterprise, or undertaking in spite of counterinfluences, opposition, or discouragement; steadfastness; a willingness and commitment to complete cycles of action and finish unfinished business.

One of the primary concepts that keeps you thriving is the ongoing understanding—the ongoing reminding—that as you grow in a relationship with your teen, you are engaged in a process that is ongoing. What you have learned and put into practice through the previous chapters helps you to attend to your beliefs, emotions, needs, and reactions so that you move further from chaos and deeper into connection. In this ongoing process, you need perseverance, an unwavering willingness to complete cycles of action and finish unfinished business, to continue to move toward connection—even in times of chaos.

You have likely had experiences in your life that required perseverance—graduating high school or college, entering a career, hiking a mountain, running a race, keeping your house clean, having a baby, adopting a child, guiding a child, building a house or business, getting dinner on the table, or hosting a party. These experiences are like your relationship with your teen, requiring planning, learning, practicing, and perseverance. You have what it takes to persevere with your teen. As you persevere in these experiences and with your teen, integrity, commitment, and responsibility will help you.

INTEGRITY

As a parent, you're a loving leader in your home, a foundation and example that your family will follow. You have discovered that if you are angry, your teen will respond with anger. If you are judgmental and react out of your triggers rather than a place of calm and love, your teen will in turn react to you and be shortchanged in his emotional cycle. You have also discovered that if you offer unconditional love, your teen will move toward you. If you know and offer yourself and your true emotions, your teen will be able to share herself and her emotions.

In orchestras, musicians often use the oboe to tune their instruments. The oboe is used because the pitch is secure and penetrating. Like an orchestra, each member of your family is trying to tune to the same pitch. You can be the oboe, the one your teen and family will tune to based on how secure in integrity you are. Having integrity means you practice awareness, are willing to listen to the voice inside of you, and follow through with the action the voice requires. Having integrity also means honoring yourself and honoring your word, following through with your commitments and renegotiating your commitments consciously (when necessary) so that you are truthful and honest with yourself as well as with others.

The following story is an example of a mom and her daughter having integrity with each other:

> Wendy and her daughter, Jenna, had been on a long journey together from Surviving to Reviving to Thriving. While in Surviving, Jenna used to say things to her mom such as, "Mom! Why don't you ever go to the ballet studio anymore? Your butt is getting so big, and it's just pathetic how you just let yourself get out of shape!" Wendy took Jenna's comments personally, and she often cried in response. As they moved to thriving, Jenna still commented on Wendy's weight, but she said, "You know, Mom, I'm a little bit nervous. I see you putting on weight, and I feel like you're not healthy. I'm afraid something might happen to you. I love you. Maybe you can go back to dancing or just to the gym." Wendy felt Jenna's love for her and her speaking to her from her heart, sharing the emotions behind her comments. In this space, Wendy was able to be curious about what was going on for Jenna and began making plans to get more exercise.

When you live with integrity—consistent, reliable honesty and fairness—you sound the note of your authentic truth, and that supports others who are trying to do the same. By standing for integrity, you can influence your teen and encourage her to be authentic as well. Constantly being authentic can be challenging, but it is a powerful way to influence your teen through your example.

COMMITMENT

Living in a loving relationship with your teen requires commitment. All relationships by nature have ups and downs because they involve people. In your relationship with your teen, you will make progress and come across challenges. Sometimes a leap forward in the relationship or emotional healing will bring new issues to the surface for healing. Unresolved issues naturally surface as you progress. As new challenges surface, you and your teen will have real opportunities to commit to being loving with yourself and with others.

To stay committed to your relationship with your teen and having a healthy family, realize first that relationships and healthy families evolve without coming to an end point. New opportunities for healing will help you and your teen to draw closer as you continue to practice the essentials of *Chaos to Connection*. When a healing opportunity arises, remember to:

- Use awareness to be in the present moment, to be curious, and to love yourself.
- Use support if you need it and create emotional safety for yourself.
- Be present and engage through attuning and listening.
- Love yourself and your child unconditionally in the moment.
- Commit to actions that arise out of your awareness and being in the present moment.

When your teen was an infant, you may have read a number of books about how babies and toddlers grow. But how many of these books described the great adventure you embark on when guiding a child? Having a loving relationship with your teen and growing a healthy family is an adventure! Adventures involve unknown danger and risks and promise excitement and incredible experiences. So does your relationship with your teen! To continue on the adventure, commit to the adventure with yourself and your teen now, especially if you are experiencing joy. When stress comes, your commitment will carry you through.

SUSTAINING RESPONSIBILITY

Sustaining responsibility for your emotions and needs will also help you to persevere. Through your practices in the essentials of *Chaos to Connection*, you have learned that you are responsible for your emotions and fulfilling your needs. In the past, when you tried to control your teen's behavior, you put the responsibility for your emotions and needs on your teen. Before you grew your emotional safety and unconditional love, you may have withdrawn your love based on your teen's behavior. Remember when you started realizing that feeling good, happy, and loving did not depend on your teen's behavior? That was when you started taking responsibility for your emotions and needs.

As you continue on the adventure with your teen, when your teen's behavior triggers you, be willing to take full responsibility for your emotions. Own them. You will find that your responsibility and ownership of your emotions empowers you. You move from being a victim to an empowered person who is secure in her integrity, able to bring awareness to her hurt, and able to move through an emotional cycle back to calm. Such ownership of emotions also reinforces your love for yourself and your teen. You continue to move beyond the question of "Who is right and who is wrong?" to "How can we heal right now?"

Your perseverance in heart-centered parenting will draw you closer to your teen. As you persevere, your relationship with your teen will start to look like the following example:

June and her son, Gavin, had been on a long journey together moving through Surviving, Reviving, and Thriving. While Surviving, June would walk in and see the messes that Gavin had left for her to clean, and all she could focus on was her belief that he was lazy and disrespectful. Acting out of those beliefs, she grounded Gavin with the hope that he would start cleaning up his messes. The more controlling she got, the more Gavin acted out and made even bigger messes. Pretty soon, June and Gavin communicated through a power struggle, and they were each determined to prove the other wrong. The house felt like a war zone, and each was out to win at all cost.

As they began moving toward Reviving, June was honest with herself about her feelings, taking responsibility for her anger and her need to control. When she would see the messes and feel the anger rising up, instead of acting out on Gavin and trying to control him, she began to sit with her anger. She saw the power it evoked in her. Instead of using that power to control Gavin, she began to use that power to inform her of her own needs. She began to see how overwhelming it was to be a single parent and take care of everything on her own. Every time she saw the mess, June decided to reach out to Gavin and to connect with him instead of nagging him, focusing more on the relationship than on the mess.

June started enjoying her son again, and in the process she noticed that he began to clean up more often. As they entered Thriving, they both began to see their relationship as a priority and began spending more time together, expressing their enjoyment and love for each other. June persevered in practicing the essentials and remained committed to her relationship with Gavin. Through their open communication, June was able to share with Gavin how a clean house supported her in feeling more relaxed. Gavin was able to hear her and also express his need to still be reminded about what he could do to help. Together they decided to spend 10 minutes a day cleaning up so things wouldn't get too overwhelming. They turned on the music, worked together, and connected with each other.

Continue to persevere in the *Chaos to Connection* essentials with integrity, commitment, and sustaining responsibility. You will continue to grow as a person, healing old wounds and making new strides in relationships. As you come alongside your teen, guiding him, your teen will also continue to make strides in himself, his life, and with you. The work you have done opens wide a door to an amazing and healthy family system where each member can express and be herself, and each member has the support she needs for healing.

COMMON CHALLENGES

You have learned so much and grown so much, and you will always have room for more growth. This is wonderful and, at the same time, not so wonderful. You may come across some of the common challenges of perseverance, including regressing into Surviving, fatigue, and challenges to your integrity.

Living in a loving relationship is a process, and stressful times will continue to arise. You may find yourself and your family slipping into behaviors that look like Surviving. Remember that such stress and emotional hurt results from wandering from the present moment back to your fears, shame, and judgment. When such stress arises, use your awareness, support, and safety to be in the present moment. Offer your loving presence to yourself and your family. Reviewing the emotional cycle in Chapter 2: Safety and the essential of presence can provide you with support.

Just as you may fall off the connection bandwagon, your partner or your teen may fall off the bandwagon. This will no doubt cause stress and possibly trigger you. As with other behaviors, remember that you take full responsibility for your emotions and needs. While your partner or teen experiences chaos, you can take care of yourself and provide healing, unconditional love. Be present with your partner or teen while they move through the emotional cycle.

If you find yourself getting worn out, despairing even, when stress arises, this is a good time to do a Wellness Check. Taking care of yourself physically gives you the strength and energy to take care of yourself emotionally, which in turn helps you to take care of your teen. If you feel like you can't handle something stressful in the moment, take a break and take care of yourself.

A final challenge that you may come across is having integrity. As you persevere in connecting to your teen, you need to sound the note of authenticity and stand for integrity and the authentic expression of who you are. Your teen will want to do the same (perhaps with more courage than you). Having integrity and expressing yourself authentically is not always popular or easy. You will find people who are threatened by, disagree with, or shame you and your teen for doing so. Remember that your integrity is integral to you and to your teen's thriving, regardless of others' responses. Find support from those who love you unconditionally to help you through such times.

On the other hand, if you find yourself offended by someone or by your teen's integrity, this can be a wonderful learning and healing moment for you. What in that person triggers your response? What does it remind you of or evoke in you?

- Perseverance is a willingness to complete cycles of action and finish unfinished business.
- Perseverance requires integrity, commitment, and responsibility.
- Having a healthy family is a journey and an adventure requiring perseverance.

KEY LEARNINGS

1. Find something that you and your teen find adventurous and do it. The adventure can be close to home: driving through a new neighborhood, finding new places to shop, trying a new ethnic cuisine or restaurant or food. Or the adventure can be further away: a trip to a new city, state, or country.

2. Review the recommitment letter you wrote in Chapter 4: Presence. Update it if you have new reasons, priorities, or changes. If you didn't write a letter, write one now. Include why you are practicing the *Chaos to Connection* essentials, why this is a priority, and make a list of what's moving and changing.

"In the long run we shape our lives and we shape ourselves. The process never ends until we die. And the choices we make are ultimately our own responsibility."

ELEANOR ROOSEVELT

9

VISION

vi·sion *(noun)*: the act or power of imagination; to picture to oneself; envisioning a new family organization based on collaboration and organized around awareness.

While you have been working on yourself and your relationship with your child, you have set the foundation for vision—having excitement about and looking forward to what the future holds for your family. Do you remember how you thought of the future when you were Surviving? You likely felt fear and dread, captured by your teen's present behavior into thinking the future would be terrible. You may have lived just day to day, unable or unwilling to think about the future. As you have learned, when you are in high stress, you can do little besides respond to the present situation, due to circumstances and how your brain is engaged.

What a shift you will begin to see in your family when you are Thriving! All of the practice that you have had in the *Chaos to Connection* essentials, all of the focus you have paid to the present moment actually brings you to a new view of the future. You now have the opportunity for vision, continuing to create family relationships with intent and with love. You have confidence that you are capable of accomplishing goals with your family. This new vision is based on collaboration and organized around awareness.

As you are starting to have a vision for your family, surrender, creativity, and alignment with your heart are important.

SURRENDER   When you practice awareness and presence, you let go of futurizing, creating stories about the future based on your teen's behavior. If your teen tells you he smoked pot, you prevent your mind from jumping into the future and reacting to the idea that he will become an addict living on the street. If you find out that your teen has started having sex, you do not react out of the fear that she will become pregnant in the future. Such thinking about the future is detrimental to your relationship with your teen and places your triggered emotions between you.

Your vision for your family considers the future but in a positive way, with your heart and mind surrendering to the present moment in complete acceptance of what is. To surrender, remember that unconditional loving is enough. You do not need to control. With this in mind, as you think about your family's future, do so with love in mind. What will be loving for everyone involved, what is devoid of control, what would interest others in your family? How can you act on your vision in a way that each person can have his or her own experience?

When you are thriving, you are able to let other people in your family co-create your family's vision. In the past, you may have been afraid to ask your teen about his future because of his emotional response or because you feared his answer would be bleak. You may have avoided talking about the future with your parenting partner because there was already too much to handle in the present. Now you have a new opportunity for creativity in your family.

As you co-create a vision for your family, creativity can present opportunities for more love and fun within your family. Tap into your and your teen's creativity by:

- Sharing stories about your childhood or your child's younger years.
- Allowing your authentic creativity to shine and inspire your teen.
- Turning off your own inner critic about what are good and bad ideas.
- Thinking outside of the box and doing what inspires you.
- Joining your teen when she lets her creative juices flow, whether it be with music play lists, clothes shopping, redecorating, video games, or driving around.

Remember that teens are often constrained by how they think they need to look, feel, and act, and that it is easy for them to lose touch with their genuine ability to relax and have fun. As you co-create, you will find new ways to connect over ideas, vision, and the actions you take.

CREATIVITY

Your vision for your family and the excitement about the future that you have discovered are a result of practicing the heart-centered essentials. Because of your practice, you have aligned with your heart. Initially, your actions, thoughts, and words may have been reactions to your teen's behavior, to triggers and old wounds; but now, through awareness you have brought your heart, body, and mind back to your true self. You have uncovered your heart. And you haven't stopped there! You uncovered your heart and discovered how to share it with your teen and your family. You have also

ALIGNMENT WITH YOUR HEART

aligned your parenting with your heart. You are now parenting from the heart, which is a place of unconditional love.

When your parenting aligns with your heart—heart-centered parenting—you are able to have vision for the future. Your triggers brought your past experiences into your present moment, and through awareness, the emotional cycle, and forgiveness, you have been able to let those experiences go. You understand your past and where it has led you, but now your past no longer decides your future. Just as you created a Grace Gap in which to respond to your teen free of your triggered feelings, you have now created a Grace Gap in which to envision your future free of your past.

You also have a new sense of boldness. In aligning with your heart, you have thrown off stories about your world and uncovered truth about who you are, about love, and about how you can act. You have come to a place of truth, and truth from within is impossible to resist. As Soren Kierkegaard wrote, "The truth is a snare: you cannot have it, without being caught. You cannot have the truth in such a way that you catch it, but only in such a way that it catches you."[1] You have been caught by the truth of yourself, and you will be bold as you move forward with that truth. Your boldness will help you to be proactive in addressing stressful or potentially stressful situations. You will also find that you aren't fearful of your future but look forward to it. For now you are truly creating the future you want and know is possible.

COMMON CHALLENGES

As exciting as having vision is, you will still have challenges, though you may view most of them as opportunities in disguise. You will find you can slide back into Surviving and Reviving. As much as you have worked to remove old stories about feelings and to be in the present moment, your mind will still create stories about your experiences and feelings. Remember to practice surrendering, a very conscious effort to stay in the present moment, and have awareness. You may find that you slip into judging your experiences, including the new ones that you have in Thriving. Continue to review all the essentials, so you can be present in the moment and surrender.

With the demands of day-to-day living, it is easy to get stuck in a routine with your family. Remember to use creativity with your family and to bust out of the box. You have the skills now to try new things and to be confident that you can handle stress that may arise. Doing new activities will continue to renew your relationship with your family.

KEY LEARNINGS

- Vision is imagining a new family organization based on collaboration and organized around awareness.
- Surrender, creativity, and alignment are key to co-creating your family's vision.
- You are living heart-centered parenting.
- When you are Thriving, you have a new excitement and boldness about your future!

PERSONAL PRACTICES

1. Write down exactly what your ideal vision is regarding your relationship with your child. Be detailed and specific. Now write a list entitled: What would I need to do this? Who would I need to be to make this vision happen? Brainstorm daily for one month. You don't have to commit to doing anything on the list, but let your creativity flow and see what emerges naturally from the process.

2. Find ways to connect to your community through family volunteer opportunities, inviting families into your home, or getting to know members in your faith community. It can be powerful and healing to see your family work together in the community.

3. Discover ways to enjoy your teen and your family's company. Get input from other family members and go out and play as a family. Have each family member take turns choosing an activity for the family.

4. Engage the storytelling that may start in your family about what life used to be like, the good and bad experiences. Find humor in talking about the past. When you can comfortably talk about the past, storytelling can be healing, insightful and a comfortable way to do so.

"A rock pile ceases to be a rock pile the moment a single man contemplates it, bearing within him the image of a cathedral."

ANTOINE DE SAINT-EXUPERY

CONTINUING ON

As you finish this book, we want you to know that you are not concluding or coming to an end, but just beginning an incredible journey with your family. And what a journey it is! From a world of chaos and powerlessness, you have moved into a world of connection and empowerment. Not only is your family life less chaotic, but you feel more open and have a greater understanding of yourself. You are unconditionally loving your child and becoming the parent you always wanted to be. You can handle changes and even chaos in your life and find a way to connect in the midst of the chaos.

We have faith that you will continue to love yourself and your child and to enjoy your thriving family. You will be continuing on in heart-centered parenting and continuing to use the essentials, those basic and indispensable pieces of building and maintaining connections:

- Awareness
- Safety
- Support
- Presence
- Engagement
- Guidance
- Forgiveness
- Perseverance
- Vision

When your family is Thriving, the *Chaos to Connection* essentials really click. What you have been practicing begins to feel natural because the essentials are natural. Your practices have deconstructed your old belief systems, and you have returned to a place of unconditional love, where behaviors are messages and feelings are only feelings. The essentials have enabled you to view your teen with a heart lens rather than a mind lens.

You were designed for this love and, at your core, have always been capable of it. Continue on in loving your teen with all of your heart. You have worked hard and deserve to be where you are.

We want to leave you with two thoughts as you continue on. You have in the course of *Chaos to Connection* learned how to express your unconditional love. Unconditional love is true love, a feeling we greatly desire in our human life and the kind of relationship we seek with other people. The term "true love" has two of the most meaningful concepts in human emotional life—love and truth. True love illustrates that without love there is no truth and without truth there is no love. When you are connected to your heart, it is easy to tell the truth. Conversely, it is difficult to tell the truth if you are not connected to your heart. If you can connect to true love, then every relationship you have will be transformed, beginning with the relationship you have with yourself.

Finally, our dream is that heart-centered parenting transforms families and communities. As you and your family flourish, you may develop a desire and ability to share *Chaos to Connection* outside of your family, to teach and guide other parents in heart-centered parenting. This is a natural and wonderful outgrowth of Thriving. With more connection and less chaos at home, you can turn some of your focus to other families and your community. We encourage you to follow your heart and to share with others by:

- Doing what you do with your teen with other people. They will feel your unconditional loving presence and feel they can open up to you.
- Providing a safe emotional place—being a support person—to your partner and other parents who need help.
- Sharing the *Chaos to Connection* essentials and practices with other parents or a small group of parents.

You may find that guiding others in heart-centered parenting is as much a blessing to you as it is to others. We know it has been for us.

Every person craves the deep connection of true love. So much of human life is a result of unrequited love and our failed attempts to get love. Each family—each person—that practices heart-centered parenting reawakens a true loving relationship. If you have been around someone who gives true love, you know it is infectious. You feel it. And by receiving it, you learn how to give it to others. Deep sharing opens the door to, even evokes, deep sharing in other people. Each of you who embraces true love becomes another brick in the foundation for a better world. You now have the essentials to change your family and to change the world.

We have faith in you.

Thank you for all the work you have done for yourself, your teen, your family, and your community. Continue on in true love.

"Love, whether newly born, or aroused from a deathlike slumber, must always create sunshine, filling the heart so full of radiance, that it overflows upon the outward world."

NATHANIEL HAWTHORNE

INDEX

CREDITS

DAVID HERZ, MA

Director of Therapeutic Services, President and Founder, Vive

As the founder of Vive and Director of Therapeutic Services, Dave leads Vive mentors and parent coaches in their application of the Vive Approach. He takes great pleasure in ensuring that the services delivered by Vive practitioners are of the highest quality, and that practitioners are each engaged in their own process of personal and professional growth. Dave has an MA in Education from the University of Colorado, Boulder. As a psychotherapist, he has worked with kids and families as a teacher, counselor, therapist, mentor, and coach for more than 20 years. He has been a rabid Cubs fan for over forty years and plans to be there with his dad and sons when they win the pennant…soon. Dave's roles as son, father of three teenagers (two boys and a girl), and husband are what keep him both humble and deeply passionate about his work with parents and young people. Dave's passion is to help young people find the courage and inspiration to move toward responsible, productive, joyful young adulthood, while helping parents engage this process with less pain and more hope.

MICHAEL BEHMER, MA

Director of Product and Media Development, Vive

Michael's passion is helping young people, especially those who are labeled "at-risk," their families, and their communities, nationally and internationally. Combining business and project management experience with clinical experience, Michael now directs the transformation of Vive's therapeutic model and practitioners experience into powerful tools for families. Michael has a degree in Marriage and Family Therapy and has worked with youth and families in private practice, therapeutic groups, residential treatment, wilderness therapy, crisis debriefing, and family systems restoration for over 18 years. He has worked with community leaders to restore families and communities nationally in New York City's Harlem and the Mississippi Delta, and internationally in Russia, Sri Lanka, Myanmar, Haiti, and China. Michael lives outside of Boulder, Colorado with his wife and two children (who always have more to teach him about parenting) and in his free time enjoys playing with his family, biking, fly fishing, snowboarding, writing, and enjoying the bounty of Colorado's natural wonders.

ANDREA DINDINGER ACH, MA, MFT

Therapeutic Team Leader, Vive

Andrea is full of life, and it shows. Her passion for working with others is evident through her life experience, which has been rich with a variety of positions and personal growth. Her experience ranges from working as a high school counselor and a therapist in day treatment centers, to providing therapy to individual adults, youth adolescents, and couples. She has been a part of Vive as a parent coach, mentor, and therapeutic team leader since 2006. She earned her MA in Counseling Psychology from California Institute of Integral Studies and is a licensed Marriage and Family Therapist in the state of California. Andrea believes that the single most important thing she can do to get through to the kids is to be really curious about them—truly interested in who they are.

LESLIE POTTER, CERTIFIED ALAYA PROCESS PRACTITIONER/MASTER'S LEVEL TRAINING

Director of Training & Parent Coach Support, Vive

Leslie is one of the foundational personalities at Vive. In 2004 she joined Vive as a parent coach, creating and implementing Vive's powerful parent-coaching model. In addition to delivering nurturing support to hundreds of Vive parents, Leslie's passion is teaching and training her colleagues in the heart-centered model. She is also the founder of Pure Joy Parenting based in Boulder, Colorado and has been in private practice for 19 years as a Certified Alaya Process Practitioner, a master's level body-oriented psychotherapy. Leslie's greatest adventure and passion is parenting her daughter, who awakens her daily to the merits of "unconditional" love for herself as well as her daughter. Together they continue to remind each other that only love is real.

ROHINI ROSS, MA

Parent Coach, Vive

Rohini has a special ability to come alongside parents in a spirit of deep compassion and practical support. Her work has focused on helping parents take care of themselves and meet their own needs so they have more of themselves to give to their children and the family as a whole. Rohini has used her gifts providing Vive services since 2006. She received her master's degree in Counseling Psychology with a Certificate in Consciousness Health and Healing from the University of Santa Monica, and she is presently an intern pursuing her licensure as a Marriage and Family Therapist in the state of California. Rohini is passionate about parenting, and her biggest teachers are her two daughters.

WILLOW RUBIN, MA, MFT, LPC   *Therapeutic Team Leader, Mentor, Vive*

Willow is truly a force at Vive. The young women she mentors, as well as the practitioners she leads, feel empowered and motivated when they are in her presence. She began working with at-risk youth in 1996 in Boulder, Colorado, while studying for her master's in Contemplative Psychotherapy. After graduating in 1999, she worked for Boulder County Mental Health Center providing home-based family and individual therapy. Now a Licensed Professional Counselor and a Marriage and Family Therapist, Willow promotes a holistic and integrated approach to therapy and holds the vision that with help, families can change patterns and heal from past wounds.

KEVIN PATRICK MCCARTHY

Kevin has been writing for 25 years. More than 50 of his essays have appeared in national publications, including *The Chicago Tribune* and *The Bloomsbury Review*. His trade books, *A Natural History of Hot Springs* and *The Eulogies*, will be published in 2010. In 2007, he won Denver Mayor John Hickenlooper's Vonnegut Appreciation Competition.

ALEXA VAN DALSEM, MA

Alexa Van Dalsem is a grant writer for a Colorado non-profit, Alternatives for Youth, which provides educational support to at-risk youth, and a writer with her company, Relational by Design. Her other writing includes short stories, poetry, a personal blog, and most recently, scripts for the *Chaos to Connection* videos. Her grant writing has provided for an expansion of services in the last three years for Alternatives for Youth, and her writing has appeared in *Ruminate Magazine*. In her free time, Alexa enjoys reading, gardening, playing with her family, and spending time in the great outdoors of her home state, Colorado.

A special thank you to Amy Lowe, Jeni Breezely, and Andrea Zimmerman for their work as editors. We greatly appreciate Amy's contributions as an experienced prose editor for *Ruminate Magazine*, her love for the *Chicago Manual of Style*, and her experience as a mother; Jeni's contributions in organization, her passion for heart-centered parenting, and her experience as a mother; and Andrea's willingness to edit the final draft.

REFERENCES

INTRODUCTION

1 National Youth Anti-Drug Media Campaign. Keeping Your Teens Drug-Free: A Family Guide. Parents: The Anti-Drug. http://www.theantidrug.com/pdfs/resources/general/General_Market_Parent_Guide.pdf.

2 Michigan Department of Education. What Research Says about Parent Involvement in Children's Education. Michigan. gov. www.michigan.gov/documents/Final_Parent_Involvement_ Fact_Sheet_14732_7.pdf.

CHAPTER 1: AWARENESS

1 Autism Asperger Publishing Company. The Process of Sensory Integration. AAPC. www.asperger.net/SensoryChap1.pdf.

2 Weaver, Jane. 2006. Can Stress Actually Be Good for You? msnbc.com. http://www.msnbc.msn.com/id/15818153.

3 Cannon, W.B. The Wisdom of the Body. New York: Norton, 1932.

4 Gruenewald, Tara L., A.R. Gurung, Laura Cousino Klein, Brian P. Lewis, Shelley E. Taylor, John A. Updegraff. 2000. Biobehavioral Responses to Stress in Females: Tend-and-Befriend, Not Fight-or-Flight. Psychological Review 107, (3): 411-429.

5 LeDoux, J. The Emotional Brain: The Mysterious Underpinnings of Emotional Life. New York: Touchstone, 1996.

6 Flaxman, Greg and Lisa Flook, PhD. Brief Summary of Mindfulness Research. UCLA Semel Institute. http://marc.ucla. edu/body.cfm?id=38&oTopID=38#summary.

7 Ibid.

8 Tang, Y., et al. 2007. Short-term Meditation Training Improves Attention and Self-regulation. PNAS 104 (43): 17152-17156.

9 Davidson, R., et al. 2003. Alterations in Brain and Immune Function

10 Lutz, A., et al. 2008. Regulation of the Neural Circuitry of Emotion by Compassion Meditation: Effects of Meditative Expertise. PLoS One 3 (3): 1-10.

11 Discovery Health. The Same Responses That Once Helped Our Ancestors Can Hurt Us Today. http://health.discovery. com/centers/stress/articles/response/response.html.

12 Adapted from Three-Minute Dose of Meditation. O, The Oprah Magazine. http://www.oprah.com/article/ omagazine/200812_omag_meditate.

13 Adapted from Relaxing into Awareness. Seishindo.org. http://www.seishindo.org/practices/relax_into _awareness.html

CHAPTER 2: SAFETY

1   Discovery Health. The Same Responses That Once Helped Our Ancestors Can Hurt Us Today. http://health.discovery.
    com/centers/stress/articles/response/response.html.

2   LeDoux, J. The Emotional Brain: The Mysterious Underpinnings of Emotional Life. New York: Touchstone, 1996.

3   Frankl, Viktor. Man's Search for Meaning. Boston: Beacon Press, 2006.

CHAPTER 3: SUPPORT

1   Gruenewald, Tara L., A.R. Gurung, Laura Cousino Klein, Brian P. Lewis, Shelley E. Taylor, John A. Updegraff. 2000.
    Biobehavioral Responses to Stress in Females: Tend-and-Befriend, Not Fight-or-Flight. Psychological Review 107,
    (3): 411-429.

2   Bornstein, Marc H., et. al. Handbook of Parenting: Volume 2, Biology and ecology of parenting. Mahwah, NJ: Lawrence
    Erlbaum Associates, 2002.

3   Search Institute. 40 Developmental Assets for Adolescents. http://www.search-institute.org/developmental-assets-tools.

4   Brazelton, T. Berry. Touchpoints. Cambridge, MA: Da Capo Lifelong Books, 1992.

CHAPTER 5: ENGAGEMENT

1   Mercer, J. Understanding Attachment. Westport, CT: Praeger, 2006.

CHAPTER 6: GUIDANCE

1   National Institute of Mental Health. Teenage Brain: A Work in Progress. National Institute of Mental Health. http://
    www.nimh.nih.gov/health/publications/teenage-brain-a-work-in-progress-fact-sheet/index.shtml.

CHAPTER 9: VISION

1   The Papers of Søren Kierkegaard, vol. 11, part 1, sect. 352. (Ed. by P. A. Heiberg and V. Kuhr, 1909).

Definitions are from Vive definitions and Merriam-Webster's Dictionary.